101

Great Answers

to the Toughest

Job Search

Problems

101
Great Answers
to the Toughest
Job Search
Problems

By
Ollie Stevenson

CAREER
PRESS

101 GREAT ANSWERS TO THE TOUGHEST JOB SEARCH PROBLEMS

ISBN 1-56414-158-6, $11.99

Cover design by The Gottry Communications Group, Inc.

Printed in the U.S.A. by Book-mart Press

To order this title by mail, please include price as noted above, $2.50 handling per order, and $1.00 for each book ordered. Send to: Career Press, Inc., 180 Fifth Ave., P.O. Box 34, Hawthorne, NJ 07507

Or call toll-free 1-800-CAREER-1 (Canada: 201-427-0229) to order using VISA or MasterCard, or for further information on books from Career Press.

Library of Congress Cataloging-in-Publication Data

Stevenson, Ollie, 1945-
   101 great answers to the toughest job search problems / by Ollie Stevenson.
     p. cm.
   Includes index.
   ISBN 1-56414-158-6 (pbk.)
   1. Job hunting--Handbooks, manuals, etc. I. Title. II. Title:
One hundred one great answers to the toughest job search problems.
III. Title: One hundred and one great answers to the toughest job
search problems.
HF5382.7.S745 1995
650.14--dc20

                                                   95-3834
                                                     CIP

Acknowledgments

I thank God for being blessed to write this book, and for all the following individuals He placed in my path to help bring about its successful completion:

Dr. Lois Frankel who said "You have to write a book."

Dr. Marilyn Parker for providing research avenues.

All the wonderful people whose stories are mentioned.

Cecilia Lopez and John Gleason for invaluable proofreading and critique of my original attempts.

Kim Terry for his much needed technical assistance.

Sinara O'Donnell for mentoring each step of the process.

Jean-Noel Bassior for helping to secure my agent.

Michael Snell, my agent, for helping to develop a winning proposal.

Betsy Sheldon, my editor, for helping to shape a winning book.

and

My children, David, Kylie and Fernando, for their very special patience and support.

Contents

Introduction   **13**

Chapter 1   **I don't know what I want to do**   **15**

1.1   Follow your natural talent   15
1.2   Don't sell yourself short   17
1.3   Find the right fit   18
1.4   Discover your unique talents   20
1.5   Discover your success pattern through accomplishments   20
1.6   Set your career goal   24

Chapter 2   **I don't know how to get started**   **37**

2.1   Plan to succeed   37
2.2   Key steps for achieving your career goal   38

Chapter 3   **I'm afraid**   **45**

3.1   I'm not qualified   45
3.2   I've never really worked anywhere else   46
3.3   An issue of confidence   47
3.4   Fear of success   48
3.5   Attitude test   49
3.6   Get a new attitude!   49

Chapter 4   **I've been laid off**   **57**

4.1   Layoffs don't carry the stigma they once did   57
4.2   What to say when you've been laid off   58
4.3   How to address the layoff on your resume   59
4.4   Network your way to your next job   60
4.5   Networking letters   63

Chapter 5   I'm female   69

5.1   Overcoming the invisible obstacles   69
5.2   Job hopping as a result of spouse's relocations   71
5.3   Back into the work force, after years of absence   71
5.4   "Just because you're a woman," they may ask...   72
5.5   Getting the salary you deserve   73
5.6   Some good news...   74

Chapter 6   I'm too old   81

6.1   Leave age off the resume   81
6.2   Making your "old" resume youthful   83
6.3   Overcome age objections during the interview   83
6.4   Be prepared to handle challenging questions   89

Chapter 7   I'm too young   91

7.1   Turn extracurricular activities into job applicable experiences   91
7.2   A resume with the impact of 10 years' experience   92
7.3   Network your way into job opportunities   93
7.4   Interviewing skills for the young job seeker   95
7.5   Difficult questions that might come up   97

Chapter 8   I'm a minority   101

8.1   Focus on skills and achievements, not ethnicity, in your resume   101
8.2   What the interviewer can't ask   102
8.3   What the interviewer might ask that may be legal—but may signal prejudice   103
8.4   You don't get the job—what can you do?   104
8.5   What to do if you believe you have a discrimination case   106

Chapter 9   I have a disability   109

9.1   Americans with Disabilities Act (ADA): The basic points   109
9.2   Workers with disabilities find more acceptance in the work force   111

| 9.3 | Handling the interview and employment process | 112 |
| 9.4 | Organizations for assistance | 114 |

Chapter 10 I don't have a degree   **117**

10.1	On the job and back to school	117
10.2	Check into your company's tuition reimbursement program	118
10.3	Those who succeeded—without a degree	119
10.4	Market yourself without a degree	121

Chapter 11 I haven't worked in years   **125**

11.1	Translate nonpaid experience into marketable skills	125
11.2	Build self-confidence through practice and preparation	126
11.3	A resume that positions you as a professional	127
11.4	Do's and don'ts for the interview	128

Chapter 12 I can't find a job in my field   **133**

12.1	Step in and fill an existing need	133
12.2	Expand your network	134
12.3	Broaden your thinking	134
12.4	Don't label yourself too narrowly	135
12.5	Get your foot in the door	136
12.6	Create your own opportunities	136

Chapter 13 I'm a technical person   **139**

13.1	How John got his resume past personnel	139
13.2	Chronological versus functional resume	140
13.3	Dress to impress	143
13.4	Interviewing	143

Chapter 14 I've made mistakes in the past   **147**

14.1	If you were fired once...	147
14.2	If you've had a long history of job failures...	148
14.3	If you have a criminal record...	149

| 14.4 | If a negative reputation prevents you from advancing in your company... | 150 |
| 14.5 | A problem resolution model | 152 |

Chapter 15 I want to make a career change   **155**

15.1	I know what I want to do—but I need more education	155
15.2	I know what I want to do—but I need experience	156
15.3	I know what I want to do—but there are no openings	157
15.4	You're ready for a career change when...	158

Chapter 16 I need to relocate   **161**

16.1	In search of better job opportunities	161
16.2	Where to find the jobs	164
16.3	Relocating with the help of an agency	164
16.4	Rewriting your resume for relocation	166
16.5	Interviewing long-distance	167
16.6	They offered me a job—but they want me to relocate	168

Chapter 17 I don't know how to get a fair salary   **171**

17.1	Do your homework	171
17.2	Is the salary fair? Consider these factors	172
17.3	A salary cut may be imminent when...	173
17.4	Revealing salary information: When is the right time?	174
17.5	Responding to salary information requests in ads and applications	175
17.6	Responding to salary information requests during the interview	176
17.7	Negotiate your salary like a pro	177

Chapter 18 I don't know whether to accept the offer   **183**

18.1	Ask for time to consider the offer	183
18.2	Make sure you know what you've been offered	183
18.3	Get the offer in writing	184
18.4	Negotiate the offer	184

18.5	When you're interviewing with more than one company	184
18.6	Accepting the offer	186

Chapter 19 I want an alternative to 9-to-5   **189**

19.1	Home-based business	189
19.2	Telecommuting—a logical move	190
19.3	Freelancing	191
19.4	Working as a "temp"	192
19.5	Independent contracting	192
19.6	Consulting	193

Chapter 20 I haven't found a job yet   **195**

20.1	Turn rejections into learning experiences	195
20.2	Make changes!	196
20.3	Widen your net	197
20.4	Ask your contacts, friends and co-workers for advice	197
20.5	Go to the experts	198
20.6	Don't be too hard on yourself	199
20.7	Be good to yourself	199

Chapter 21 Where can I get more help?   **201**

21.1	Sources of employer information	201
21.2	Additional help in preparing	205
21.3	Business and professional organizations	206

Postscript   **207**

Index   **209**

Introduction

The purpose of this book is to provide specific answers to the toughest problems that are preventing you from having the career you want.

I have included examples of job-hunting problems reflecting a wide spectrum of occupations and situations so that this book will be useful for you whether you are an hourly worker, secretary, technical professional or executive. It will help if you are: trying to decide on a career direction; trying to advance in your career; unemployed and seeking a new job; seeking a different job within your company; seeking a career change; or trying to decide if you want to start your own business.

The key to successfully achieving your career goal rests first in knowing that you are a valuable person with a unique combination of skills and talents to offer the world, and then implementing a plan to identify and maximize that talent.

The real-life stories in this book typify problems that people just like you have overcome in order to achieve their career goals. The solutions represent the actual steps they took to remove roadblocks to their career success.

For example, you will learn how a duplicating operator overcame a lack of confidence, sold his skills and got a job. You will read about a clerk who progressed to the executive level in her company and was contacted by officials in Washington, DC, to serve on one of the President's special committees. And you will discover how others chose career alternatives that gave them greater freedom and improved their lifestyles.

Those committed people overcame their roadblocks and used talent, perseverance and a plan to achieve their dreams—and so can you.

Over the past 10 years of conducting workshops and counseling thousands of people about their careers, I have discovered that the most common roadblocks people face are fear of failure, not knowing what they want to do and not knowing how to compete in the new and changing business environment.

Instead of implementing a deliberate career plan, most people just respond to whatever job happens next. If they are looking for work, they usually start the process using the same methods they used when they looked for their last job—which may have been 10 years ago. The trouble with that, is that the entire job hunting process and business culture have evolved several times in the past ten years.

Instead of seeking a company that will provide 30 years of security with an automatic career track, it's now necessary to take responsibility for identifying your talents and planning a career path that may have to be developed by changing companies several times.

The solutions in this book will help you to meet the challenge of developing your own career and competing in the new environment by showing you how to eliminate roadblocks to:

1. Assessing your accomplishments and success patterns so you can develop a career goal.
2. Approaching the job market with confidence.
3. Writing a winning cover letter that will get your resume read instead of overlooked.
4. Developing a winning resume that will be an effective advertising tool focusing only on the positive attributes you bring to the job.
5. Having a positive, productive interview by setting it up before going in.
6. Getting the right salary every time.
7. Maximizing your progress within your present company.
8. Deciding if you are ready to be a contractor or start your own business.

Since this book focuses on the roadblocks encountered in a comprehensive career development process, only a few resumes and letters are provided as points of reference, so if more examples are desired, I recommend the books suggested in Chapter 21.

Finally, if you use the suggestions in this book and work as hard and as smart for yourself as you have for your past employers, I guarantee that you will overcome all the roadblocks to success and get that job leading to the career of your dreams.

Chapter 1

I don't know what I want to do

There is a saying that if you don't know where you're going, any road will take you there. "Going with the flow" may work in some situations, but it is probably not the best way to get on a satisfying career track.

Identifying a career goal strictly by a past job title, or pursuing a certain type of job because "that's what I've always done," are not good motivators for a fulfilling career choice. You're not likely to be satisfied in a career that has been based solely on influences like: the job was there and you needed one; your friends were in the same type of work; your parents encouraged you to pursue that line of work because they wanted you to have security, or it's the same line of work they pursued.

A satisfying career must be developed around your own desires, something you can put your heart into. When you examine your past work experiences and extracurricular activities, you'll discover a success pattern of skills, traits and knowledge around which to establish a career goal that you can commit to. Once your talents and strengths have been identified, you should market that information to prospective employers—in order to get on a career track that will provide true satisfaction.

1.1 Follow your natural talent

Gloria worked 13 years for a mid-sized management consulting firm before she felt stagnant in her job. Even while experiencing significant personal trauma she had been able to manage her career and receive several promotions. But after a few years as a director with a staff of 10 people, the challenge had worn off and the job seemed routine.

She had never consciously set goals for her career; instead, she had met the challenge of whatever job she had and took on more responsibilities when she got bored. Her desire for change was more for stimulation than for promotional consideration.

While she saw herself as a capable worker, she did not believe she possessed any special combination of talents and skills that would make her especially marketable. But cutbacks in her department decreased the opportunity for growth and forced her to take stock of her career. She decided to leave the company. She wasn't sure of what to do next, so she committed herself to doing some serious self-examination and exploration of career opportunities.

First, she asked several friends and peers for their perceptions of her capabilities. They saw her as an excellent manager and implementor. She was reminded that while traveling for the job 30 percent of the time, she organized and carried through her own wedding, attended by 500 people, and simultaneously supervised the care of an invalid parent. Her organizational and delegation skills allowed her to juggle many responsibilities at the same time. Her friends also expressed admiration for her perseverance in getting two of her staff members promoted and for using her networking contacts to help one of her associates get placed in the right business enterprise for his skills.

In assessing her career, she felt good about being in a position to help others realize their goals. She was stimulated by the challenge of simultaneously handling several demanding tasks. Although her need for achievement was somewhat satisfied in her current job, she felt a need for more variety and control.

After realizing that a full-time position within a company structure would no longer permit the variety and freedom she needed, she decided that it would be best to work with several companies providing service in her area of expertise.

She used her contacts to locate opportunities (see Section 4.4). She negotiated a contract with one company for a limited number of hours per week and partial benefits. With this contract she was able to do a lot of the work at home. The assignment gave her more control of her time and allowed her to negotiate contracts with two more companies, which added to the variety and stimulation she needed.

Her new career as an independent contractor allowed her to use her professional knowledge, natural management capability and networking contacts to maximum advantage. She ultimately made more money and was able to work at her own pace, in a more satisfying and rewarding manner. (See Section 19.5.)

Like Gloria, it's important for all of us to determine our success patterns as revealed through our accomplishments. Since we often ignore those talents that come easily to us, we need to get feedback from others to help identify skills and options we may be overlooking. (See Section 1.4.)

But be sure to listen to your own inner voice regarding your values and interests. Even if all your family and friends, who adore your homemade bread, urge you to open up a bakery, don't do it if you know you'd never be satisfied with that sort of lifestyle.

In order to determine your career direction, you also need to research the market to determine the best niche for your skills and then set your goal (see Chapter 21).

1.2 Don't sell yourself short

Beverly worked for a major oil company in Texas as a marketing representative. She had a good education and an excellent work history. After seven years with the company, she was notified that her position, along with 800 others, was to be eliminated within three months. She immediately started sending out resumes and received many opportunities to interview, but she seemed unable to secure a position.

One day, she visited a career counselor the company had hired to assist the displaced employees. After 15 minutes with the counselor she realized she had been selling herself short, and she had to make a decision about what career direction she wanted to take.

The counselor said her impression of Beverly, when she walked in the door, was of a very sophisticated, extremely well-dressed businesswoman. She even commented that Beverly looked like an ad for a successful female executive. Based on her review of Beverly's work history she felt she had extensive experience, qualifications and accomplishments that Beverly was not drawing attention to. During her interview with Beverly, she discovered her resume was primarily based on her last title and old job description, which did not take into account her growth and responsibilities, which had increased significantly.

The counselor let Beverly know that she had probably intimidated the potential employers who interviewed her. Her observation was confirmed when she found that several had said she was overqualified for their job and some employers had even indicated that she seemed capable of handling *their* position.

Until her discussion with the counselor, Beverly had not realized the impact of her accomplishments. Now she had a dilemma. She knew she enjoyed the type of work she had been doing but now had to decide at what level she wanted to work. Should she just go for a "job," limit the qualifications on her resume and downplay her skills and presentation of herself in interviews, or should she go for a higher level position and commit to a career? While she had handled heavy assignments in her former position, ultimately the major responsibility had rested with someone else. At a higher level, she realized she would be more accountable and probably have to travel and alter her personal lifestyle.

After thinking the situation over for a few days and discussing the matter with friends, she decided that moving forward was her best alternative. She did not want to repeat the frustration of working at a level beneath her capabilities, so she decided she would rather deal with the demands, increased responsibilities and risks of a higher position.

The counselor showed Beverly how to compose a functional resume for seeking a higher-level position. Within three months, she secured the best job of her career—as a regional sales manager for a manufacturing firm—and she learned not to sell herself short.

1.3   Find the right fit

Be true to yourself

Rita was laid off from a job in the credit and collection department of a large retail organization. She had done her work well, because she enjoyed helping others and resolving problems, but being a credit representative was not what she wanted to be.

Eight years prior, recently divorced with a child to support, she had followed the advice of friends and accepted the credit job, because it was the first one offered. Over time and with pay increases, she developed a sense of comfort with its security, if not completely with the work. The layoff served as a catalyst for her to rethink her career direction.

The company provided a generous severance package, so she had some time before she was forced to accept another job. With her experience and references, Rita knew that she could get another position as a credit representative, possibly one leading to credit manager. Then she could save the severance pay for a rainy day. Her other alternative was to finish college and obtain her nursing degree—a lifelong dream.

After discussing the matter with the career counselor the company had provided, she decided that she needed to grasp the opportunity to pursue the career she really wanted. After all, how often would she have a lump sum of money and a window of opportunity like this? Her parents agreed to let her and her child live with them so she could attend school full-time. She got a part-time job and used the severance pay to supplement her needs while she worked toward her degree, and she felt the satisfaction of knowing that she was finally doing what she wanted to do.

A closed door may mean an open window

Bill worked as a systems consultant for a major manufacturing company for 15 years. For 13 of those years, he tried every approach possible to move into a management position within the company, but was unsuccessful. His superiors said they viewed his services as valuable, but for reasons unknown to him, he was continually passed over for management positions.

He became frustrated. He saw no opportunity for moving up and saw the dream of reaching his financial goals and securing the kind of lifestyle he wanted dissipating as each year passed.

Confronted with this lack of upward mobility, Bill had to reevaluate his situation and decide what he really wanted in his career. If his options were limited at his current company, should he consider applying for higher positions at other companies? When he talked with some of his associates in other companies, he noticed they were experiencing some of the same frustration he was. He reasoned that if he switched companies, he might experience a further delay as he took time to prove himself and fit into their political arena.

Next, he wondered if he should quit and start his own consulting business. Three of his peers had done that, and two years later one of them was struggling to make ends meet and the other two were looking for jobs back with a corporation. They had neither planned well, nor anticipated some of the pitfalls of being in business.

Bill realized that a higher-level job in his company or another company was not the real issue for him. The real issue was how to maintain his current stability and still move forward financially and professionally. He decided to strike a middle ground in his next career move. He opted to maintain the security of his current position while marketing his consulting business on the side. He reasoned that when he had built a reputation and clientele as a consultant, then he would feel more secure about leaving the company.

He started a networking effort that paid off quickly. Within a short period of time, he was approached by a nonprofit organization to design a system for them. That project became the catalyst by which he was able to get other business. By keeping his job while developing his business, Bill was able to implement a low-risk plan that gave him what he really wanted—not so much to be a manager, but to have financial security and career growth. So the failed promotion attempts ultimately led him in a direction that was even more rewarding.

1.4 Discover your unique talents

You discover your unique talents by looking in the following three areas:

1. **What you used to dream about becoming when you grew up.** Example: Janice wanted to be a teacher, missionary and philanthropist at various points during her childhood. She was outgoing and always willing to help others. That trait continued into her adult life with her positions in personnel administration and community-supported, fund-raising activities for worthy causes.

2. **Feedback from others.** Example: Janice was always complimented for being a persuasive communicator, outgoing and very helpful to others. It had even been suggested that she would be an excellent teacher or psychiatrist because of her people skills.

3. **Analyzing your accomplishments.** Example: As a young adult Janice organized an entire community to help support a political candidate. Later, because of her leadership skills, she was offered the job of directing a community action agency that facilitated improvements in the community. And in her career she was drawn to and selected for jobs where she helped develop the skills of others and was able to help many people advance and overcome psychological barriers to their success.

Summing it all up, Janice's *natural talent at analyzing people and their skills*, combined with her *ability to influence* and her *desire to help,* led her full-circle to a position as a social worker, which encompassed the main aspects of her original dream.

1.5 Discover your success pattern through accomplishments

Accomplishments are the cornerstone to discovering your pattern of success and in communicating your skills and abilities. They are the actual, quantified examples of what you have done and are the best predictors of your capabilities. Accomplishments show:

- What unique qualities you bring to a task
- How well you've carried out your tasks
- A success pattern of the skills you typically use
- Whether your skill pattern supports your career goal

Three people could have the exact same job, title and responsibilities, but each person would bring a unique combination of talent and skills to the task.

John, Carol and Stuart worked for different companies in the insurance industry and were competing for an office management position in a rival firm. Their previous responsibilities and educational levels were similar.

John and Carol prepared resumes that listed their job titles and included in-depth explanations of their responsibilities, but Stuart was chosen for the interview because he prepared a resume that piqued the employer's interest.

He assumed the prospective employer had similar positions to those he'd had, so rather than fill up his resume with responsibilities, he listed the following accomplishments and supported those with only the titles and company name of his former jobs:

- Coordinated, edited, formatted and implemented 12 new lines of insurance policies during a one-year transitional period while maintaining daily work flow of typed policies and endorsements.
- During a nine-month period, supervised reformatting and conversion of more than 1,000 insurance documents to a new IBM-based system, simultaneously retraining four videotypists to use a specialized system and WordPerfect program.
- Managed a department of 14 persons for five years. Obtained upgrades for three staff members and was commended by divisional management for maintaining vigorous production schedules and high-quality standards.

These accomplishments tell a lot about Stuart's likelihood of being a success in the new position. They demonstrate his management, supervisory and technical skills, plus they indicate that he is highly productive and a motivator of people. Listing responsibilities would only have indicated what he was supposed to have done. They would not indicate how well he carried out his responsibilities.

What activities would be considered accomplishments?

- Achieve more with the same time, materials, potential, etc.
- Achieve the same with less time, money, etc.
- Make things easier.
- Attain something for the first time.
- Resolve a "panic" problem with little or no ramification.
- Increase profit, reduce costs, increase sales, enlarge market.

- Improve quality—such as higher product reliability, better employee performance.

- Improve relations—such as more satisfied customers, better employer/employee relations, improved teamwork replacing conflict.

- Create more significant, quicker or smoother flow of information, leading ultimately to better decisions.

- Reduce time in operations, increase productivity.

- Achieve a new technological process or administrative procedure that previously had not been available.

How are accomplishments formulated? A well-formulated accomplishment statement has two parts, namely:

What you did (not what steps you took to get it done, or what technique you applied—those are the "glad-you-asked-me-that" interview elements). For instance:

- Managed the team that was able to obtain crucial parts for the Apollo program against a tight deadline.

- Reorganized and set up a new filing system for an engineering department of 165 professionals.

The benefit or result derived from it by an individual, employer, organization, group, etc. It's important to *quantify* the results. In other words, instead of saying "increased productivity," say "increased productivity by 42 percent." Instead of saying "reduced costs," say "reduced costs by $64,000 a year."

To be convincing to an employer, your accomplishments should be formulated in a language that is relevant to the job requirements of the prospective employer. Have someone in the industry check them to make sure you're using the right "buzzwords."

Here are just a few examples of accomplishment statements:

- Installed a complete accounting system, by department, in a large agency, decreasing operating costs by 25 percent.

- Created a profit-and-loss statement, by product, resulting in substantial increased sales of the more profitable products.

- Managed a professional group in creation of a sales organization, after identifying a $300M market.

- Conceived a new management information services procedure that provided management with vital daily operation reports of the preceding day's activities.

- Created and administered more than 1 million lines of free newspaper and magazine publicity, helping to maintain top television ratings.
- Established the necessary sales and service organization "from scratch" in the midwestern and eastern market area, leading to 75 percent of total sales now derived from those markets.
- Saved millions of dollars in possible damages and prevented financial embarrassment to the company by discovering potential bankruptcy of a key supplier.

Action verbs for accomplishment statements

The following partial list of action verbs may help you get started with preparation of your accomplishments.

achieved	established	mediated
administered	evaluated	motivated
analyzed	executed	negotiated
arranged	expanded	operated
built	experienced	organized
clarified	formed	originated
conceived	formulated	overcame
constructed	founded	performed
consulted	generated	pioneered
controlled	halved	planned
converted	headed	prepared
coordinated	implemented	promoted
correlated	improved	provided
created	increased	reduced
delegated	initiated	researched
demonstrated	innovated	simplified
designed	inspired	solved
detailed	installed	sparked
developed	integrated	succeeded
devised	interviewed	tailored
directed	invented	transformed
discovered	justified	trebled
doubled	keynoted	unified
earned	led	verified
effected	maintained	wrote
engineered	managed	

How to use your accomplishments

On a sheet of paper, list as many accomplishments as you can think of. An ideal number would be 15 to 20 spanning your career and extracurricular activities; but at least five are necessary to show skill and success patterns.

The accomplishments may be selected from positions you have held and from activity sources you've been involved with, such as community groups, associations and school activities. Remember the format should be *what you did (action)* and how someone or some group *benefited (result)*.

Analyze your accomplishments for the skills and success pattern they reveal (See Exercise 4 in the following section.) An ideal job for you would encompass the skills revealed in that pattern.

Accomplishments should be used in your resume, cover letters, marketing letters and interviews to help sell your skills.

1.6   Set your career goal

Complete the exercises on pages 25-35. You should use this information to help you set a career goal and decide on your next job objective.

Knowing what you want to do is the essence of obtaining a career you'll be happy with. But you cannot come to grips with that knowledge without some time and effort directed toward a thorough self-analysis. That analysis is especially important if you have not changed jobs or careers in more than five years. Although the process has to be initiated internally by you, it should definitely include input from others who know you and have observed demonstrations of your skills. Their objective observations will be valuable and save you from trying to perform the whole task by yourself. And, more importantly, they will be able to point out positive characteristics that you may be overlooking. Your self-esteem will be raised as your analysis reveals the true value of your achievements. That knowledge will give you the confidence to set your goal and clearly communicate your capabilities to prospective employers. When you know where you want to go, it will be easy to choose the right road to take you there.

Exercise 1.

How am I perceived by friends, business associates, etc.?

Summarize the general themes from comments requested from several sources. Try to convey the information in positive terms. For instance, comments like "You're so picky," "You're so hard to please" could translate to being detail-oriented or having a high standard of performance for self and others.

_____

_____

_____

_____

_____

_____

_____

_____

_____

_____

_____

_____

_____

_____

_____

_____

_____

_____

_____

_____

Exercise 2.

I feel good about...

List several major accomplishments. Pick the top three or four accomplishments from your life that you are most proud of and that most closely align with skills you would like to use in your new career. (See "How to use your accomplishments" in Section 1.5.)

_____

_____

_____

_____

_____

_____

_____

_____

_____

_____

_____

_____

_____

_____

_____

_____

_____

_____

_____

_____

_____

_____

Exercise 2 (continued)

Exercise 3.

My most developed skills are...

On the following pages, list your top five accomplishments from Exercise 2. Analyze each accomplishment separately, and write beside it the skills, traits and knowledge that are revealed. Those that are repeated most often are your most developed skills and should be part of the basis for your new career. Refer to the following list if you need some help with this process.

Leadership Skills

Initiating	Self-motivated
Decisive	Directing others
Seizing opportunities	Inspiring others
Innovative	

Managerial/Administrative Skills

Handling conflicts	Conducting meetings
Accurate work	Organizing and planning
Convincing others	Flexible
Solving problems	Grasping situations
Learning new procedures	Delegating work
Handling multiple tasks	Control

Interpersonal Skills

Making friends	Making a good first impression
Accepting criticism	Understanding others' feelings
Not critical	Communicating ideas
Cooperating	Seeking input from others

Traits

Persevering in completion of difficult tasks
Committed to attainment of goals
Most effective working independently
Team-oriented in handling functions
Creative approach in application of knowledge

Example:

Accomplishment	Skills
Proposed and implemented a new marketing program which increased sales by 300% in six months.	Initiating Directing others Solving problems Communicating ideas Creativity

Exercise 3 (continued)

1. _____
_____
_____
_____
_____
_____
_____
_____
_____

2. _____
_____
_____
_____
_____
_____
_____
_____
_____
_____

3. _____
_____
_____
_____
_____
_____
_____
_____
_____

Exercise 3 (continued)

4. _____

_____

_____

_____

_____

_____

_____

_____

5. _____

_____

_____

_____

_____

_____

_____

_____

_____

_____

_____

_____

_____

Exercise 4.

How I see myself

Your strengths and areas for improvement. List skills that have been the most beneficial in accomplishing your goals and those you need to develop more because you have experienced problems due to a deficiency. For example: You have been most successful being in charge of new projects because of your ability to conceptualize and motivate others, but you need to improve at being patient with others who may not grasp concepts as quickly as you.

_____

_____

_____

_____

_____

_____

_____

_____

_____

_____

_____

_____

_____

_____

_____

_____

_____

_____

_____

Exercise 5.

Job satisfaction is derived from...

Be critical. The objective of this exercise is to spot both positive and negative patterns in order to get a position that will be a source of satisfaction, and to avoid repeating a negative experience.

_____

_____

_____

_____

_____

_____

_____

_____

_____

_____

_____

_____

_____

_____

_____

_____

_____

_____

_____

_____

Exercise 6.

My personal values are...

List the top four. Focus on the values that are most important now and those you believe will be a priority for the next five years. The following list will help you with that process.

Personal values

Accomplishment. I have contributed to my work, my world.

Stability. My life is stable and in balance.

Spontaneity. Not feeling restricted, feeling I can have fun and be myself.

Health. Living a physically healthy life; exercising, eating properly.

Belonging. Feeling loved, wanted and needed by my family.

Spiritual. Growing spiritually, having religious conviction and involvement.

Interpersonal. Being liked and respected by others.

Communication. Developing good communication skills.

Expansion. Knowing that I am growing intellectually.

Insight. Learning to accept my strengths and weaknesses, to like myself.

Security. Not having to worry about financial obligations.

Development. Working on improving myself.

Extracurricular. Enjoying hobbies and outside interests.

Others. List any value that is important to you that is not shown here.

_____

_____

_____

_____

_____

_____

_____

_____

_____

_____

_____

_____

Exercise 7.

My career goal is...

Compare the skills necessary for your ideal job against the skills demonstrated in past jobs and activities. If you will be using similar skills, your career goal is probably on track. If not, you may need to rethink your goal. For instance: Your goal is to be a lawyer because you enjoy using your investigative mind and you like helping others. Since your background has been in hotel management, which has permitted you to develop your problem-solving ability and fulfill a need to help others, your skill experience is in line with your career goal.

_____

_____

_____

_____

_____

_____

_____

_____

_____

_____

_____

_____

_____

_____

_____

_____

_____

_____

Exercise 8.

My next logical job objective is...

If your next job is not the ideal one, it should at least put you closer to your career goal by allowing you to use the same skills you'd use in your dream job. For instance, if you desire to be an attorney because of your analytical ability and you need to get a law degree, a next logical step would be joining a company that has a tuition reimbursement program and where you could get a job using your analytical skills.

_____

_____

_____

_____

_____

_____

_____

_____

_____

_____

_____

_____

_____

_____

_____

_____

_____

_____

Resolutions

1. Set aside some time for self-examination, to identify your career goals.
2. Determine what you love to do, what you're good at.
3. Get feedback from others—friends, family, co-workers—to get their perceptions of your skills and accomplishments.
4. Consider your values and lifestyle when you think about your goals.
5. Do some research about a few of the career directions you're considering. Find out everything you can.
6. Don't limit yourself. Just because you haven't had the education, training or experience in a particular area doesn't mean that career isn't attainable with a plan.
7. Identify those accomplishments you're most proud of, whether they were achieved on the job, in school, in a volunteer capacity or as a hobby or personal interest.
8. For each accomplishment, identify the result achieved.
9. List your accomplishment statements, using action verbs.
10. Complete the career goal exercises in this chapter.

Chapter 2

I don't know how to get started

Perhaps you know exactly what you want to do with your life. Whether it's to become a nationally recognized anchor person, an advertising executive or a rodeo clown, you can see where you want to be. The problem is, you just can't figure out how to get there—your career roadmap seems tangled with winding roads, dangerous curves and dead ends.

Too often, our journey toward our career dream gets stalled far before we reach our final destination—if we ever get started at all! Knowing where you want to go is crucial in achieving career success, but it's only the first step. You then have to get started in the right direction. And that requires a variety of actions from you, including initiative, attitude, commitment and a lot more. Read on to discover how you can get off the starting block and take the first steps toward your career goal.

2.1 Plan to succeed

Kim's eyes sparkled as she described how she convinced the chef at one of the most famous restaurants in Los Angeles to give her the first apprenticeship in that restaurant's history—and he gave it on her terms. The training and experience would later prove invaluable in helping fulfill her heart's desire of opening her own restaurant.

Kim was committed and deliberate in working toward her goal. Since college, she had made the most of her MBA and strong analytical skills by developing a moderately successful career as a financial analyst in the banking industry. She had accepted the bank position because she believed the financial experience would aid her later in managing her own restaurant.

While maintaining her position at the bank, she used every spare occasion to work toward her goal. Two or three weekends a month were spent trying new recipes and having friends taste the fare. That made her house a popular spot. Several times a month, Kim and her boyfriend would also eat at popular restaurants around the city to study the food and unique characteristics that made these restaurants successful.

The event leading to the apprenticeship was when Kim extended compliments to the chef, who later came out to thank her. During their conversation, she expressed her desire to be a chef and own her own restaurant. She also mentioned what an honor it would be to assist him in that restaurant. He offered her an apprenticeship during the conversation that followed. Kim still had a look of surprise and pleasant disbelief on her face as she told the story. She kept saying, "I still can't believe this!"

But believe it, she should! Kim's coup wasn't entirely a matter of luck. She had built a positive foundation, a sure path that led toward her career goal. Her enthusiasm, involvement, commitment and determination put her in the right place at the right time to receive the apprenticeship that would surely give her career a jump start.

Kim conveyed to the chef the same enthusiastic attitude about cooking that she showed others while telling the story. Despite holding down a full-time job, she made herself available to work for the chef as much as possible, and maintained her enthusiasm—looking at late hours and weekend work as an opportunity rather than a duty. He couldn't resist helping her. Kim had demonstrated with her positive attitude that she was a winner—and people like to help winners.

Whether looking for a job, seeking a career change or planning to start your own business, like Kim, your plan should include the key steps outlined in the next section.

2.2   Key steps for achieving your career goal

Step 1. Choose to have a positive attitude.

Whether you choose a positive attitude or a negative one, your choice will have a significant influence on the outcome of your plan. That's right! If you choose to let the negative attitude of fear dominate your thinking, you will succeed in bringing about what you fear most. If you choose to let the positive attitude of faith dominate your thinking, you'll succeed in accomplishing more than you hoped.

Kim's attitude had a positive influence on every aspect of her career change. It was demonstrated in her compliments to the chef and her quickness in grasping an opportunity to further her career. His response to her positive attitude was the offer of an apprenticeship.

If you are happy about your career goal and able to admire similar talent in others, then you have a positive attitude. If you always have an excuse for why you cannot get moving with your career, then you may have an inappropriate career goal for your skills, or you need to change your attitude. (See the Attitude Test in Chapter 3.)

Step 2. Choose a goal based on your talents.

One of the fundamental keys to achieving success in a career is basing it on those natural skills you like to use. Kim was building her career on talent and skills she enjoyed, skills that were easy for her and that seemed to come naturally. She was willing to maximize those skills so that she could ultimately work full-time at something that gave her personal satisfaction.

If you have natural aptitude in an area, it will not be hidden from you or anyone else. You will often be complimented for those skills—for instance, "Kim, you are a wonderful cook," or "Let's let Kim cook the food for the party, then we know it will be good," or "We can always count on Kim to come up with a fantastic dish," or "What a unique recipe. How did you make this?" These kinds of comments are all evidence of a special talent in cooking.

If your career goal is based solely on money and a talent that has not been demonstrated to you or others, then you are likely moving in the wrong direction, and your chosen career might seem difficult to achieve and ultimately prove unfulfilling. (See Section 1.4.)

Step 3. Choose a goal you can commit to.

Kim was committed to owning her own restaurant, so she was also willing to assume the responsibility of being a business owner. (See Chapter 19.) If owning a restaurant had not been the right option for her, she could have set a different goal, like being chef at a restaurant or catering on the weekend, for example.

Kim was also willing to commit a lot of personal time and effort to prepare for achieving her goal. A key test for determining if you have set a positive career goal is how much of your personal time you're willing to give without getting paid up front.

Are you willing to do volunteer work? Go back to school? Take an internship, or accept an entry-level position in order to gain the experience or contacts you might need to further your goals? Would you agree to "moonlighting" to earn some skills necessary?

Put your career goal to the test by asking yourself these questions. If you answer "no," then your commitment may be questionable. (See Section 1.6.)

Step 4. Be competitive.

Not only must talent be refined and developed, it must be put in the best setting to produce a quality result. Kim was not satisfied with simply having a *talent* for cooking and a *desire* to own a restaurant; she wanted her restaurant to be the best. She researched the industry and other restaurants so she would know what worked, what didn't and how her talent fit in. One of the most important reasons to be competitive is to ensure that you will succeed and yield a high return for your effort. The better you know your market, prospective employer and the other people you are competing against, the easier it will be to show the uniqueness of your product and service and fulfill the special niche that will translate to success for you.

Whether starting a business or seeking a job, you need to be able to show characteristics that make you unique in your field. This can be done by analyzing your success pattern (see Section 1.5) and by comparing your capabilities with people who already do what you want to do.

Step 5. Use many avenues to reach the goal.

You need to be prepared to "play the numbers game" and use all viable strategies to reach your goal.

If your goal is to start your own business, you'll need to develop a solid business plan. (See Section 21.2.) Before finalizing your plan, it would be a good idea to explore several avenues for interim marketing of your product or service. In Kim's case, some alternatives to her plan of an apprenticeship prior to opening her restaurant could have included: selling a specialty item through a restaurant; contracting to handle the food service at a small restaurant one afternoon a week; catering lunches to office workers within a limited geographic location; or starting a partnership venture with a well-known pastry house that already has an established clientele. An alternative strategy might even prove more lucrative than the original idea. At the very least, the alternative strategy could help build a clientele for when the restaurant opened.

If your goal is to seek a job, statistics validate that networking has been the most effective job search strategy for the greatest number of people. But, as noted below, it is not the only strategy that works:

Clint had worked for 15 years when he was laid off and had to look for a job. He figured he had four months before he experienced a serious financial problem. He developed a plan for getting a job that incorporated every approach he could think of, read about or was suggested to him.

- He prepared two versions of his resume and had several colleagues and a career consultant give him feedback on them.
- He started responding to ads in his local newspaper, *The Wall Street Journal* and professional publications that he read regularly.
- He made a list of all the people he knew and started setting up information interviews so he could find out what was really happening in the market.
- He let his associates know of his availability.
- He signed up with two search agencies.
- He started attending the chamber of commerce meetings in his area as well as surrounding areas.
- He did some research at the library to develop a list of companies so that he could target ones that might benefit from his services. He sent a letter to each company and followed up with a call to set up a networking interview.
- At a friend's suggestion, he developed a few networking contacts by volunteering his services to a community-based youth group that was heavily supported by the business community in his area.

Finally, his efforts started to pay off. Two weeks before his self-imposed deadline, he had two job offers on the table and was scheduled for an interview with a third company. One offer came from a networking contact that he traded calls with 18 times before they actually had a meeting. The second offer came from a company to which he had sent an unsolicited resume. The interview with the third company was in response to an ad. He finally had gotten results because he made a plan that included using every viable strategy available to him.

Sometimes a career strategy might require making a lateral or backwards move like Joanne did when she left her permanent secretarial position within a corporate law department and decided to work as a temporary secretary for as many private law firms as she could so she would have an opportunity to network into a paralegal position. It took her 18 months to finally land the paralegal opportunity she wanted. Sometimes opportunities come easily. But usually you have to be willing to make many calls, follow up on many leads, network with many people and just generally use *many* avenues to secure the job.

Step 6. Know how much money your skills are worth.

Using your talents in your career should be financially rewarding as well as personally fulfilling. In deciding on a career direction, you need to consider your lifestyle needs and feel comfortable that your choice will support those needs. For instance, if you have a desire to take care of small children, but your love of children doesn't outweigh your desire to clear six figures annually, you may want to reevaluate how you want to meet your financial goals. Would you be willing to limit your income to $20,000 annually to run a day-care center? Or are you committed to both your career and lifestyle goals enough to plan on running *five* day-care centers to accomplish an annual income of $100,000? As part of your decision-making process, it is important to have knowledge of income levels for your skills.

The best source for salary information is from individuals who are doing the kind of work you want to do. This can usually be obtained by asking them what kind of income *range* a person can expect for that type of work. As long as you let them know you are seeking general information and not their specific salary or income level, you'll probably not have a problem obtaining the information.

A second source of income information is through an association for that function. The *Encyclopedia of Associations*, available at public libraries, provides a listing of associations nationally. If an association chapter is not in your location, you can write to its national office and obtain some information. A third source of information is the *American Almanac of Salaries*, which is updated biannually and is also available at the public library.

Step 7. Be able to pass a five-second interview.

Whenever you communicate with someone about your career goals—whether in a casual networking conversation or an informal interview—the exchange should be treated as if it were as important as an interview. In today's "pay for performance" culture, prospective employers want to know what you can do, your level of motivation and your personality traits. In talking about her week-end cooking experience to the chef, Kim conveyed enthusiasm, demonstrated she was highly motivated and showed she was a hard worker with her willingness to work two jobs. (See Section 7.3.)

Step 8. Check often to make sure you're on the right track.

If you are just starting your career journey, even if you do everything right, job offers may be limited. At first, you may feel the need to just accept a job because it's there and you need one. Even so, it is important to have a goal, so that you will be able to maximize every opportunity you receive.

The greatest benefits of a first job may be the opportunity to establish a work ethic, meet people you can network with later and who may help you refine your career goals, and spend some time gaining supplemental training. Those benefits will carry over well into whatever career you are pursuing.

As you grow in experience and take jobs along the way, you may be in a position of deciding between offers. Some will be more profitable than others in boosting your career in the right direction, so as you move closer to your goal you will need to start weighing experience against dollars. For example, if you are working toward becoming a film producer, the assistant position for a nonprofit in-house production department might be better than a higher-paying but totally unrelated position. The better opportunity will stand out as the one that best satisfies your overall goal. (See Chapter 18.) In Kim's case, the most important aspect of the apprenticeship was the opportunity to enhance her long-term goal. Since she had a day job, salary was not an important issue.

Step 9. Have a flexible plan for growth.

As soon as you obtain your new job, start planning your next career move. Following her apprenticeship, Kim had her sights set on a management position in restaurant operations. She planned to gain that experience at another restaurant.

Kim accepted that her career and its growth was her responsibility. She was practical and hardworking. She wanted to keep her "day job" until she felt comfortable about the change. She realized that it would take her some time to succeed in her new career, so she made cautious financial moves that resulted in her having to work hard but allowed her to be less fearful about the change.

Kim effectively employed good business strategies to successfully reach her goal.

The first few steps of any journey can be difficult and uncertain, especially when you have to learn that obstacles, delays and hard work are part of the process. All successful people know this. They learned it the same way that you will. But, like them, you will succeed in your endeavor if you endure, see the process as refining your talent and keep your eyes on the target.

Resolutions

1. Develop a positive attitude.
2. Choose a goal based on your talents and interests.
3. Commit yourself to your goal.
4. Be willing to compete to achieve your goal.
5. Use many avenues to reach your goal.
6. Know how much your skills are worth.
7. Be prepared for the five-second interview.
8. Check often to make sure you're on the right track.
9. Have a flexible plan for growth.

Chapter 3

I'm afraid

Whether or not you have the skills, experience and education to get another job, your reaction might still be the same: You may be blocked from moving forward or accomplishing anything, paralyzed into inactivity. It is human nature to be afraid of the unknown, even for people who seem to be positive about most things. But, just like learning how to write a resume, interview properly or set realistic career goals, there are methods for building your confidence and moving past fear to accomplish your goals.

3.1 I'm not qualified

Sam lost his job as a duplicating press operator after eight years and feared he was not skilled enough to secure another position. He hid his fear behind a "I don't have anything to offer, so why try?" mask.

He was 45 minutes late the first day of the job change workshop the company had provided for its displaced employees. He told the instructor it was because he had a hard time finding the building and that it didn't matter if he got there late anyway, because he didn't think the program would do him any good. He didn't think he would find another job because he felt his skills were not sufficient to compete for another job. He stated that the only work experience he'd had prior to his last job was eight years with the military, and he couldn't reenlist because he was too old.

The rest of that day, he worked along diligently with the other participants in using the self-assessment methods to identify his strengths and success patterns. As a result, he identified several ideas he had implemented on his former job to improve production and efficiency. After writing out those accomplishments, he became more hopeful of his chances for securing a position. At the end of the day his comment was, "Hey, I really did make things a little better around that place." He left the workshop with a new self-confidence.

That evening the owner of a small printing company called him at home. The man said he was looking to hire a few people for his operation, and he had been referred to Sam by an associate. Sam went in for the interview that evening. Because he had just identified the contributions he made in his prior job he was able to convey that information to the owner and sell himself for the job. The owner offered him a job on the spot.

The next day of the workshop, after listening to the story, the other participants asked if he was going to accept the offer. He said, with a confident smile, "I don't know. I told him I would think about it and get back to him in a couple of days."

Sam was afraid to look for a job because he didn't think he had the skills or qualifications to land another one. After he really took stock of his accomplishments, he was able to recognize the value of his skills and experience. This gave him the confidence to sell himself to a new employer.

3.2 I've never really worked anywhere else

William's story was similar to Sam's—except he was laid off from a high-level management position with an oil company. His career with the company had started with an entry-level position 32 years earlier. He had been a real team player—a company man. But when he was let go, he didn't know how to describe what he could do.

His former title was impressive enough to make him intimidating and it also implied that he ought to have the confidence and contacts to get a job. But he was just as afraid as Sam that he didn't have anything to offer, so he also hid behind a mask of indifference. He said, "I don't really have to work, I'm only looking to do some volunteer work where I can help others out." In reality he didn't know how to develop a career goal, because he had never thought he'd have to compete outside his former company.

After using the assessment methods outlined in Chapter 1 and gaining an understanding of the significance of his achievements, he felt confident in his ability to identify career options and explore avenues for obtaining a position.

In both of these situations, the individuals overcame their job hunting fear with knowledge. Sam identified his achievements through the help of a workshop, while William discovered his achievements through self-assessment exercises. No matter what your situation, if your fear is that you aren't qualified to find a job, it's important for you to get in touch with reality and recognize that you have indeed gathered some impressive skills and accomplishments that can be valued by new employers. Whether you must sign up for a skills-assessment workshop, work with a job counselor, talk to friends and co-workers or complete all the exercises in Chapter 1 of this book, take the necessary steps to convince yourself that you are quite qualified to land a new and fulfilling job.

Knowing how to sell yourself on resumes and in the interview is the next step. Sam was able to interview with confidence after he realized he had something to offer and William was able to approach the job market with confidence when he understood how to communicate his skills. Practice interviewing with friends and employment agency representatives. Or plan for a few dress rehearsals by interviewing for jobs for which you have a low interest. What's important is to build your confidence.

Be willing to explore opportunities that are presented and to develop others through networking. (See Section 4.4.) Networking is one of the best avenues to get a position, because it often provides a mentor who makes the introduction and therefore serves as an agent. It makes the interview process easier because the interviewer already expects to like you since they like the person who referred you.

3.3   An issue of confidence

How can I do my job when I'm scared to death?

Fred, who had been a marketing representative with his company for many years, was given a temporary assignment as manager of the marketing services group while the company was being restructured. It was his first management opportunity and a position he had desired for a long time.

At first he was extremely happy, or so it seemed. But soon panic and insecurity set in. He seemed unsure of what to do, constantly complained about the ineffective staff and generally expressed uncertainty about setting goals and managing a function that was not permanent. Consequently, he did not establish any goals or working criteria. He concentrated on the fact that at the end of six months he would be out of the position. He allowed his fear and insecurity to prevent him from functioning. At the end of the sixth month, Fred was terminated and given severance pay.

Turning a threat into an opportunity

Katherine worked for the same company as Fred as a clerk in the marketing department. She was also temporarily upgraded, moved into a management position as a marketing analyst to provide support to one of the managers on a new project.

Katherine approached the new project with zeal. She applied her clerical skills and analytical ability diligently and developed credibility in the new position. Within a few weeks she had computerized a process to capture and organize all the information relevant to the project, and by the end of the second month she had established herself as the focal point for reports and other pertinent information. She became invaluable. Her quick response to requests was highly appreciated, and she demonstrated her ability to see the big picture by anticipating and providing appropriate supplemental information.

Her commitment did not go unnoticed. During the assignment period she was interviewed and offered two other positions within the company, which she declined because she wanted to complete the temporary project assignment. She believed the experience gained would make her more marketable at the end of the project.

At the completion of the assignment, Katherine was commended highly by her superiors and was placed back in a clerical position at the same level she'd had prior to the analyst position. But within seven months she secured a promotional opportunity that was higher than the research analyst position. Within 18 months she obtained two more promotions. Apparently the word spread about her capability and her attitude. Because Katherine chose to use the analyst position to demonstrate her ability and gain additional experience, she succeeded in obtaining her goal to be promoted to a management position.

Confidence is developed by taking small successful steps toward your goal. Katherine was willing to use her new opportunity to develop skills and increase knowledge that supported her goal. In doing so, she received long-term reward. She expressed a positive attitude about her temporary assignment and was committed to it, despite the upheaval in the company.

3.4 Fear of success

When Yvette's department was eliminated at the company where she had worked for 14 years, she was surprised and pleased when management asked her to consider transferring to its Texas operation.

However, her family had a very negative reaction to the news. Their responses ranged from "You don't know a soul there" to "What if you can't afford the cost of living?" to "We won't ever see you again!"

Yvette's original enthusiasm about the opportunity quickly disintegrated to fear, not so much about her ability to handle the job but her concerns about maintaining ties to family and friends. She turned down the transfer opportunity.

Whether it's pressure from family or friends, fear of the unknown or discomfort with making a change, we often let concerns unrelated to our job performance influence our decision to pursue a satisfying career. Often, our fear is less that we'll fail and more that we'll succeed!

Examine the reasons for your refusal to move forward in your career. And once you identify your fear, confront it and attempt to resolve it. If it's unsupportive family, do your best to assure your loved ones of your commitment to them and then ask for their support in making your decision.

Be willing to at least explore growth opportunities, whatever they are. One woman ended up making a move across country to take a job in a new field. She overcame her initial fears of life changes by telling herself each step of the way, "If they offer me the job, I can always say 'no.' " Finally, when she did receive the offer, she was comfortable with the idea of change and enthusiastically accepted.

3.5 Attitude test

Your attitude influences everything. If you've just been laid off or missed a promotion, it may be showing in your attitude. In addition to the material in this book, you may need to get input from a number of sources about how the career development process works and your level of personal responsibility for attaining your goal.

The test on pages 52 and 53 will help you determine your attitude. Answer the questions and compare your answers to the results on pages 54 and 55.

3.6 Get a new attitude!

You've got to grab hold of your mind, shake out all the negative notions and start looking at the wonderful opportunities that exist for you as a result of the tremendous changes in the business world. If you've just been laid off or missed a promotion, give yourself a few weeks to get a grip on your negative emotions as a result of the loss. If you're still having a hard time getting on with your career after that period of time, then seek some professional assistance. To get out of the rut of negative thinking, use the following six-week plan to start changing your attitude by modifying your behavior.

Week 1. Fix your spiritual body.

Every morning, for at least 15 minutes, fix your mind on something positive: your ideal career; a past experience that turned out well; prayer, meditation, yoga, reading the Bible or a metaphysical book, or whatever gets you to a positive place. Do this exercise every day at the same time.

Week 2. Fix your mental body.

Start a new activity—a class, bowling, a support group, weekly lunch with two other people who want to make a job change—whatever will bolster your self-esteem. Try to participate in this activity at the same time each week.

Week 3. Fix your physical body.

Exercise. Ugh—hate it? Do it anyway, for at least 15 minutes each day. This is not for weight control. It is to help eliminate stress and free the mind. A short, brisk walk will suffice.

Weeks 4 and 5. Fix your appearance.

If you have looked the same for the past five years, it's time to change. Women, get a new hairstyle. Change your makeup (get a free makeover at a department store). Men, go to a stylist, it's worth it. Manicure your nails and reshape your mustache. And everyone should replace those outdated outfits with suits and attire that properly reflect the professional image you want to attain. Not only will dressing better improve your attitude, but those new suits will come in handy for interviews.

Week 6. Add a new friend.

Reach out. Introduce yourself to someone in one of your classes or at a professional association. Talk to your new friend about something positive. Talk to him or her about your six-week transformation. These new contacts could open doors to new opportunities of all kinds for you.

By the sixth week you should be looking good, feeling good and confident about expanding your horizons. Go for it!

If fear wore a red jumpsuit and carried a pitchfork, we'd probably all be sensible enough to avoid it. But that is not the case. Fear is usually more subtle than that. It is more often disguised in excuses, slight hesitations, procrastination, denials and anticipation of probable negative outcomes. You cannot wait for fear to leave because it never will completely. You just have to be willing to proceed forward—making positive adjustments along the way—until you accomplish your goal.

Resolutions

1. Overcome your fears of failure by identifying your achievements, using the exercises in Chapter 1.

2. Don't let panic about being out of work cloud your reactions or your ability to see good opportunities for advancing yourself.

3. Turn transitional positions at your company into opportunities to showcase talents and skills your employer may not have seen before.

4. Use every chance you can to learn new skills that could open doors to new jobs.

5. Show a positive attitude at work, even if your job is uncertain.

6. Explore all new opportunities, even if they may require lifestyle changes you're uncomfortable with.

7. Examine the reasons why you may be refusing to move forward in your career. Make sure you're not being held back by the fears of family and loved ones.

8. Develop a positive attitude through the exercise provided in this chapter. Work on your spirit, mind, appearance and attitude, and make progress toward achieving your goals.

Attitude Test

1. **You are a professional who has been on five interviews and you've been rejected each time. You believe it is because you are lacking one particular qualification. You would:**

A. Follow up with the interviewers and ask why you didn't get the job.

B. Continue to interview, but don't waste time with companies or situations that are similar to those who turned you down.

2. **You were laid off three months ago. Since that time you have not been able to locate another position, although you have some leads. Your former company offers you a contract position that is almost identical to your old position. You:**

A. Decline the position. In your panic about finding a full-time position, you can't imagine working on a project and job-hunting at the same time.

B. Accept the offer while looking for another opportunity.

3. **You notice that there is a need to create a position in your department to handle certain tasks that are slipping through the cracks. You would:**

A. Suggest to management that someone should do something about the tasks that are not being handled.

B. Outline the tasks and present them to management as a promotional opportunity for yourself.

4. **Out of the blue, you are offered a position that represents everything you have been striving for, except you have to change your lifestyle and relocate to another state across the country. You would:**

A. Refuse to go and hope that another opportunity comes along that would not require such big changes in your life.

B. Investigate the opportunity. Evaluate it for its potential to help you achieve your career goal and consider the benefits versus the losses before making your decision.

5. **You need a job soon. You are getting anxious because you have already been rejected several times with the interviewer stating it is because you are overqualified. You would:**

A. Tone down your resume and your discussion of past accomplishments so you could get the next job.

B. Set your sights for a higher-level position more consistent with your qualifications.

6. **You had a salary range in mind for your next position. The prospective employer offers you a wonderful job but at quite a bit less than your minimum salary requirement. You would:**

A. Turn down the offer and hold out for what you know your skills are worth.

B. Inform the employer that you're excited about the job opportunities and would be willing to accept it if the salary met your expectations.

7. **You have performed at a high level of proficiency for years and hoped that your management would notice and give you a promotional opportunity. So far they have not done so. You would:**

A. Work harder, be patient and not rock the boat. After all, they are bound to reward your good performance eventually.

B. Bring your level of performance and your expectations to their attention and request consideration for promotional opportunities.

Answers

1. **A.** You should gather your courage and ask why you did not get the job. To continue to interview, or avoid interviews you fear will lead to rejection, and hope you eventually get a position stems from fear and denial and is a waste of time. Your time would be better spent finding out what you need to do in order to prepare yourself for the type of job you want. You'd be surprised at how much valuable information you can find out from your interviewers. In fact, you might just impress a prospective employer with your eagerness to meet his or her needs, so that you'll be called if another opportunity opens up.

2. **B.** Accept the offer as you continue to look for a better opportunity. A lot of companies are downsizing and are forced to use contract workers to help cut costs and remain competitive. Having work will more than likely ease your panic as you know some income is coming in. In addition, you'll be gathering new experience and skills as a contract worker that can be added to your resume. And you may end up enjoying your independence so much that you'll choose to strike out on your own as a full-time contractor.

3. **B.** Take the initiative to write and present the job description yourself. Usually opportunities have to be grabbed for, much like the brass ring on a merry-go-round. You may not get the job, but management will surely respect your attitude and eventually you will be rewarded for your display of initiative in some manner—maybe with a different and better job.

4. **B.** You should always investigate and evaluate any offer thoroughly before responding. Opportunities rarely come exactly the way we expect. Often they are more than what we hoped for and usually include at least one aspect that may seem a little challenging to us. A big opportunity is going to require change, and since it is human nature to resist change, our initial reaction may be negative. It is a good idea to give yourself some time to evaluate an offer objectively (if you can) against your career and lifestyle goals. You may need to get an objective viewpoint from a friend before making your final decision.

5. **B.** If you are consistently receiving feedback that you are overqualified for positions and the statements are based on your abilities rather than your former salary, then you

probably *are* overqualified and should be seeking a higher-level position.

If you are desperately in need of a job, and the lower-level positions are the only ones available, you should adjust your resume down so it only reflects the skills needed for the position you seek. But bear in mind that if you take a lesser position than your capabilities, it may prove very frustrating over the long term. It is easier to adjust up than down. So if you accept a lower position, it should be for a temporary period and you should continue to seek one that is in line with your capabilities.

6. **B.** You should always have some idea of the market value of your skills before starting the interview process. If the offer is a lot less than the industry standard and it is a job you're really interested in, you should point out the going rate for the position and try to negotiate. (See Chapter 17.)

7. **B.** Sometimes you have to speak up and let management know that you desire to progress and gain more responsibility. Point out that you believe that you have done well on your job and support your discussion with examples of your accomplishments (see Section 1.5). After that, start a discussion about the requirements for you to get a promotion. Be willing to receive more responsibility.

Chapter 4

I've been laid off

With an MBA and 22 years in a management position with a Fortune 500 company, Keith believed he had his career under control—until he received a layoff notice, along with almost 100 other employees in the company's northeastern headquarters. Not only did he agonize about telling his wife and family, he dreaded the humiliation when his friends and community found out. He eventually confided in his wife but kept the news from his many contacts in the various organizations in which he was active.

In addition, Keith panicked at the thought that he would never land another job if his prospective employers learned he was jobless. His fears caused him to pass up a number of opportunities to interview for excellent positions. "What's the use?" he'd ask his wife. "Once they find out I'm jobless, they're going to wonder what's wrong with me and take me out of the running."

4.1 Layoffs don't carry the stigma they once did

Of course, it's always preferable to be searching for another job when you're currently employed. But in a time when companies continue to restructure, reorganize and downsize their way out of employees, being laid off does not carry the stigma it once did. Major industries—including computers, oil, banking, insurance and aerospace—have reduced their staffs by thousands of talented administrative, professional and management workers. As difficult as it is to accept for the individual, the change usually is not personal. Employers are aware of this when interviewing laid-off candidates to fill positions, and they don't assume that the interviewer is at fault for his or her current status. One of the statements in the following section may be helpful in letting your family and friends know what has happened.

If you find yourself among the ranks of downsized employees, first confront the emotional issues that are sure to bombard you.

You'll likely feel humiliated and betrayed, and perhaps you'll even doubt your abilities. Thoughts like, "Maybe I really *don't* know what I'm doing in this position" and "I was just lucky to have that position. I'll probably never find another one" are bound to sabotage you.

Often, companies in the midst of a reorganization will offer employees affected by the changes some support, from counseling to help in finding jobs through an outplacement program. Take advantage of all these opportunities. Seek assistance through the employee assistance program—you need to bolster your self-esteem right now, because you have some work ahead of you to land that next job. If your company does not provide any counseling services, seek support elsewhere. Your positive mental attitude right now is crucial!

Next, take advantage of any outplacement services your company offers you. Often, a company will give generous notice to employees before they're let go. Take this time to make as many contacts and land as many interviews as possible. Your employed status, however temporary, may give you the psychological edge you need during the interviewing process. And most importantly, despite your anger and sense of betrayal, don't burn bridges with your company. You never know if conditions may change—and new opportunities might open up with your company.

4.2 What to say when you've been laid off

People usually are sympathetic to a job loss, but they don't know what to do or say. Not knowing how to react, people will usually empathize with whatever emotion you project to them. If you are angry, they will be also. To avoid an undesirable reaction, figure out how your family, friends, associates and creditors can be helpful to you before you tell them about your layoff. That way, you can tell them, move right into how they can help and skip any awkward negative reactions. Suggested approaches might be:

To family

"The company has been having financial trouble, so they have decided to cut back on some of its operations and departments. My department was eliminated. It didn't have anything to do with me personally. I'm sorry that it has happened, because I will miss working there, but I'm looking forward to a new experience, and here is how you can help..."

To friends and associates

"My company has gotten caught in the cost-cutting crunch. They've been forced to eliminate my whole division. I have some time before I have to accept another position, so I've decided to research a few industries so I'll know how to position myself before starting to look for a job. It would be very helpful to me if you could give me some information about...or if we can sit down and talk a few minutes about..."

To creditors

"I've been laid off from my company, and I want to make a temporary arrangement to handle my obligation until I get another position. I've always maintained good credit, and I want to make sure that I keep that credit in good standing. Here is the arrangement I've worked out, and I hope it will be acceptable to your company..."

To prospective employers during an interview

"The company made a decision to relocate its _____ division to _____ , and I elected to remain here, and that is why I'm seeking a new position."

or

"The current situation in the _____ industry forced the company to reduce its _____ division by _____ percent, so that's why I'm seeking a new position."

or

"The _____ function and the _____ function were combined, and the more senior (or junior) people were retained, so that's why I'm seeking a new position."

or

"The company centralized/decentralized its _____ function, and my entire department was eliminated, so that is why I'm seeking a new position."

4.3   How to address the layoff on your resume

If you are on salary continuation after leaving the company, it is accurate to show on your resume that you are still employed— because you still are, and technically your company can require you to come to work at any time while you maintain that status. If you have completely separated from the company, you may want to indicate the number of years that you were with the company in the section of your resume where you would normally show dates. For instance, if it is June 1995, and you've been laid off since April, indicate on your resume that you worked for the company from 1990 to 1995, or for six years. *Don't* include the months.

Another alternative is to leave dates off altogether and show a number of years in the summary statement at the top of your resume. For example:

• More than 15 years of experience as a credit representative.

In most cases, if you have not worked for a while, you'll probably want to include these techniques in a functional resume format. (See Section 5.3.)

4.4   Network your way to your next job

In our opening scenario, Keith was reluctant to let any of his friends and community contacts know about his job loss. He saw his situation as being a poor reflection upon himself and feared people would think badly of him. But by shutting down the communication with potential job contacts, Keith was closing off opportunities to find out about other job openings. What he didn't realize was that most people want to help and, given the chance, will come through with as much helpful information as they can.

By not using personal contacts, or *networking,* you eliminate what experts believe to be the single most productive method of gaining employment. Getting a job is primarily a social process. Knowing one person can expose you to a second and a third, and so on. Obtaining contacts or referrals from each person you speak with can provide the opportunity to talk with a large number of people and thereby significantly increase the potential of learning of job leads.

Networking can assist you with:

• Gaining job leads and information about places of employment.

• Determining stability and pay scale of a company.

• Determining current market value for your skills.

• Evaluating the possibilities for career change.

• Learning of additional contacts.

• Gaining mentors, thereby minimizing the possibility of rejection.

Make a list of everyone you know

To get started, list everyone you can think of who might have a job or can refer you to additional contacts who have jobs or know of job prospects.

Start with your Christmas card list, address book and every other source you can recall. Some other sources are:

- Professional acquaintances and associates
- Neighbors
- Personal friends
- School classmates
- Former teachers
- Former employers
- Suppliers
- Customers
- Club, community and religious groups
- Professional associations

There are individuals who may not know you personally but do know of places of employment and/or jobs. Some of these could be:

- Bankers
- Insurance agents
- Stockbrokers
- Attorneys
- College placement officers
- City officials
- Chamber of commerce members
- Real estate agents
- Retailers
- Individuals providing personal services (beauticians, barbers, bartenders)

Contact your contacts

Once your lists are complete, contact all the individuals you can. You will probably just call those neighbors, co-workers and other individuals you're friendly with. You'll want to let them know about your situation and find out if they are aware of any opportunities you might be interested in or if they can recommend some individuals you should talk to. Facilitate a relaxed atmosphere by stating you do not expect them to have a job or know about one. Some suggested dialogue follows:

> *"As part of my job search, I am contacting all of my associates in _____ organization. After ___ years with _____ company, I have lost touch with the employment market in (geographic area). I would really appreciate your input."*

or

> *"It would be very helpful for me to talk with you, as a leader in your field, about the transferability of my skills into your area."*

For those you don't know as well, you can send a letter first (see examples at the end of this chapter) followed by a phone call; or call to schedule an information interview. The objective is always to get a personal interview, because that is the only way you will be remembered. You're not seeking a job interview at this point, but rather an *information* interview—an opportunity to find out about a company, a department within a company, an individual who might have the power to hire you or about an industry in general. While there may be a job opportunity there, you're not here to *ask* for a job.

Try to establish a specific time and date for your personal interview. If at all possible, mail a resume to get there before your meeting. It is best if your contact can review it prior to your arrival.

Prior to the meeting, attempt to gather information concerning the individual and company. By arriving a little early you can listen and observe the environment in the company. Often this can be very useful input, particularly if a job situation begins to develop.

The interview itself will normally include discussions similar to these:

- Social exchange to relax the participants.

- Some discussion of what happened at your prior company.

- Questions from your contact about your experiences.

- A critique of the resume. You will probably have to initiate this discussion. Always carry several extra copies with you. Listen to and accept any comments or suggestions.

- Suggestions of other contacts.

- Recommendations of other companies or industries to pursue.

• Suggestions of other actions you should take to position yourself for the career opportunities you're pursuing.

If the interviewer requests extensive detail concerning your background, evaluate whether you are now in a potential job interview, and if and when appropriate, switch to the interviewing approaches outlined in Chapter 7.

You should always try to leave a networking interview with either a solid job lead or some other key people to approach. The theory calls for an ever-widening web of interrelated interviews. Most people are very willing to give you the names of other people you can contact. As your availability becomes known to the right people, positions will be uncovered or created.

Follow up with your contacts

Send a follow-up letter to every person you meet, thanking him or her for the time given to you (see example at end of chapter). If the contact made some suggestions or referred you to others to contact, indicate that you will let him or her know how the referral worked out. This will also serve as an opening for further interaction with the person with whom you initially interviewed.

After you start the networking process, you will generate secondary contacts through referrals from people on your lists. Although your initial contact with these referrals may be through letters, every effort should also be made to set up an interview. If you plan to cold-call on a secondary contact instead of sending a letter first, it may be helpful to have your primary contact pave the way by calling the person first.

You think you will remember who referred you and the names of all your contacts. You won't. It may be important to have this information later, so keep track of everyone you talk to. Include information about who referred you, when you made contact and notes regarding your conversation, whether a brief phone call or an information interview.

4.5   Networking letters

The letters at the end of this chapter can be used as a first step to opening communication with primary and secondary contacts and letting them know of your availability.

Resolutions

1. Don't keep your layoff a secret. Being laid off does not carry the stigma it once did, and the word-of-mouth referrals you receive could be your most important avenue to a new job.

2. If you've been given some time before your departure date, do as much as you can during that time to lay the groundwork for landing your next job.

3. Take advantage of any counseling services your company may provide its employees to deal with the stress and anxiety caused by a layoff.

4. Use any outplacement and job-hunting resources your company may offer.

5. Position your layoff in the most positive terms you can to your family, friends and community contacts, and ask for their support·and help in providing leads for other jobs.

6. Maintain your enthusiasm and a positive attitude toward your new job search.

7. Develop your network by identifying and contacting everyone you know who might be able to provide job leads.

8. Set up *information* interviews, not job interviews, with your networking contacts.

9. Keep in touch with your networking contacts, keeping them posted of your job-search progress.

10. Never pressure your networking contacts to get you a job. Remember, you're in search of *information*, which will lead you to find a job.

11. You can position your laid-off status in a positive light on your resume. Be sure not to try to cover it up, which will only make it appear as if you were let go because of poor performance.

12. If asked about your layoff during a job interview, be up front. Don't bad-mouth your former company. If you handle this right, you'll come off as enthusiastic and positive, rather than a resentful employee.

Letter for primary contact

Date

Mr. G. A. Hones
KKG Corporation
1520 Ames Boulevard
Los Angeles, CA 90071

Dear George:

It has been some time since we have gotten together. You may have heard that XYZ company has undergone a major reorganization. As a result of the restructure, my department was eliminated.

The company is being very supportive and, in fact, continues to try to find an appropriate position for me internally. However, we all agree that it would be prudent for me to conduct a thorough job campaign.

Before I start looking for a position, I would like to get some information on several industries and some guidance on salary ranges. As I consider you one of the most knowledgeable individuals in this area, I'd like an opportunity to "pick your brain" on some of these issues. I am enclosing my resume and would also appreciate your review of how my skills would fit in your industry.

I will contact you next week to set up a brief meeting to discuss avenues I might explore within your industry.

Very truly yours,

Paul Marsh

Paul Marsh

Enclosure

Letter for secondary contact

Date

Mr. Roger Smith
ASC International, Inc.
Los Angeles, CA 90071

Dear Mr. Smith:

In a recent discussion, Mr. G. A. Hones suggested I contact
you for counsel in exploring career options, since the
restructure in XYZ Company eliminated my division.

He did not imply that you knew of any specific openings at this
time but that you might be willing to help by sharing some of
your knowledge of companies in your industry and suggesting
associates or business acquaintances whom I might want to
meet. Your comments would be very helpful to me in
determining where my skills and experience should be
presented.

My background includes more than 17 years of experience in
travel marketing. Enclosed is a resume for your review.

I will call in the next few days to see if we might arrange a
brief meeting.

Very truly yours,

Paul Marsh

Paul Marsh

Enclosure

Follow-up to networking interview

Date

Mr. G. A. Hones
KKG Corporation
1520 Ames Boulevard
Los Angeles, CA 90071

Dear George:

Thank you for your courtesies on Monday. It was an
interesting and informative interview, which served to
heighten my interest in KKG Corporation. Keep me in mind if
my experience at XYZ Company can be beneficial in making
your corporation a success.

I appreciate your referral to Mr. Roger Smith at ASC
International, Inc. We have been in communication and have
a meeting scheduled for next week. I will get back to you after
our discussion.

Very truly yours,

Paul Marsh

Paul Marsh

Chapter 5

I'm female

You've come a long way, baby! But you've still got a ways to go. Corporations are becoming more "female-oriented" and are adopting what are considered traditionally female management styles, including more of a team approach. But for the most part women are still not paid equitably for the same jobs men hold, their numbers in management are few by comparison—and they're often barred from positions of real control in the running of company matters.

Why? Because the wheels of change turn slowly, and partly because women are often not socialized to compete for professional opportunities, which may mean being aggressive, taking credit for success, calling attention to themselves and demanding promotions and raises. Also, women more frequently have to handle job obstacles, such as reentering the work force after raising a family, entering the work force as an older adult because of divorce, widowhood or financial problems, or struggling with skepticism from employers who expect women to be less than committed because they have families.

While talent, perseverance and commitment can override gender, a smart woman must make herself aware of the challenges she may face in the job search process.

5.1 Overcoming the invisible obstacles

When Terry decided to switch from academia to business, she planned for success by anticipating and addressing the obstacles to each step of the process. Education wasn't a problem—she had an MBA—but she was ambitious and wanted a position of real authority and decision-making in a mid-sized to large company. Her first step was to get in the door of a mid-sized company that had a management training program. She constructed a resume that highlighted her education at a highly respected university and focused on her leadership and business skills she'd gathered in her teaching jobs and community activities. She used a functional resume and included the skills her research revealed were needed for management trainees. *Not* included were details on her personal health, physical characteristics or marital status.

Terry was called for an interview by one of the 10 companies she had approached. She knew that it was important for her to project a professional and serious image. She practiced role-playing interviews with a friend and selected an appropriate outfit to wear for the interview. Petite and thin, Terry looked younger than her 36 years. She dressed in a dark-blue pinstriped suit with a soft gray silk blouse, wore her hair in a simple French twist and opted for small pearl earrings and no other jewelry. She arrived for the interview on time and greeted everyone, from the receptionist to the interviewer, with a handshake and a smile.

As the interview proceeded and Terry was asked to "tell me a little about yourself," she kept focused on her professional achievements, deliberately leaving out any reference to family or personal life. Later in the interview, the prospective employer asked Terry if she had children. While Terry knew she didn't have to answer this question by law, she addressed the interviewer's concern. "If you are wondering whether my personal life will in any way conflict with my responsibilities on the job, let me assure you that I am a committed and dependable worker and consider my job a priority."

The interview concluded positively, and Terry was delighted to receive an offer from the company less than a week later. She expressed her pleasure in being offered the opportunity and assured the employer she would call with a response the following day. After double-checking her research notes, she confirmed that the salary offered was slightly lower than the market value for the job in the area. Armed with this knowledge, Terry called back and informed the employer that she'd be happy to accept the position if they could meet her salary requirements. After some internal discussion, the company gave her the salary she requested, and Terry eventually worked her way up to a vice president position in the company.

And they all lived happily ever after, right? Well, it doesn't always go so smoothly, but Terry did several things right in her efforts to overcome any gender discrimination and land the job she wanted. First, she focused on her achievements and skills in her resume and presented herself in a professional manner during the interview. While she was friendly and made an effort to create a rapport with the interviewer and others she came into contact with, she presented herself as a confident individual who knew her value.

During the interview, she steered clear of personal issues, again focusing on work instead. When confronted with questions about her personal status, Terry responded effectively to the interviewer's concern—which was "will you be committed to the job?" And when Terry was given an offer, she had the knowledge and the self-confidence to ask for the salary she knew she deserved.

While it may not always be this easy, it's important for women to recognize the gender obstacles confronting them in the job hunt process and take steps to remove them.

5.2   Job hopping as a result of spouse's relocations

Every year or two, Linda's husband was transferred by his company to a new location. Because he made the higher salary, she would quit her job and coordinate the move, then find another job in their new location. Landing that first job after her family's initial move had not been too difficult, but after three moves and three short-term jobs, Linda found the responses to her job queries were diminishing. She was convinced that it was because her resume drew attention to her erratic job history.

First she addressed her resume. A career counselor suggested restructuring it into a functional format, so the accomplishments could be listed together for greater impact, and the dates, which called attention to her short-lived jobs, could be left off. She provided total years of experience as part of a summary, including pertinent volunteer work. The resulting resume on page 77 at the end of this chapter helped generate the interviews that led to Linda's next job in her new location.

5.3   Back into the work force, after years of absence

Following her divorce, Maria needed to return to work, after a six-year absence, to support her two children. She had excellent qualifications and extensive experience, but she had two major concerns: Would an employer think her experience was too old and therefore not relevant; and would she be able to compete with men and younger people for the jobs she'd be interested in?

Maria prepared a boilerplate resume on her computer, which she could modify for a number of positions. She used a functional resume format so she could avoid drawing attention to her lack of recent work experience. It also allowed her to pull in the skills she'd developed in volunteer capacities. A copy of her resume appears at the end of this chapter on pages 78 and 79.

5.4 "Just because you're a woman," they may ask...

The inappropriate, and often illegal, questions you may be asked will usually revolve around your personal life, children, marital status and sometimes your ability to function in a male-dominated environment. Generally, the employer is trying to determine if you can meet the demands of the job. You always have the option of saying that the questions are discriminatory, but it is probably more beneficial to address the underlying need motivating the questions.

Interviewer: "This job sometimes requires long hours. Would that be a problem with your husband and children?"

Response: "I can assure you that I am committed to my career and have no problem with putting in the hours necessary to get my job done."

Interviewer: "Do you have children?"

Response: "I imagine you're asking me that because you may be concerned about my ability to commit to after-hours work. Let me assure you that it is my intention to more than meet the demands of my job. I have excellent primary and alternate childcare, so extra hours will never be a problem for me."

Interviewer: "Do you plan to have children?"

Response: "If you're concerned that I'm not committed to a career with your company, let me assure you that I am. I've spent a lot of time acquiring the education and skills necessary to succeed in my career, and I plan to give it the priority it requires."

Interviewer: "Most of the people in the department are men, and you know how men can be. Any problems with working with a lot of men?"

Response: "No. In my profession, I'm accustomed to working with a lot of men. We've all respected each other and have been able to work together very well (smile) and they were still able to be themselves."

Interviewer: "A lot of the staff are men; any problem with supervising that kind of group?"

Response: "None whatsoever. I believe it's important to establish performance standards that everyone understands and then evaluate them fairly against those standards. That way there are no surprises for anyone."

Interviewer: "I see that you've changed jobs quite frequently. I'm wondering if you'd be satisfied at this company."

Response: "In the past, I've made job changes because of family commitments. But I am now in a place where I can make my career a priority. I am committed to my career and believe I've made a real contribution in each job. As a matter of fact, the varied experience I've gained as a result of the changes have made me a more valuable employee because I've been able to bring new ideas to each job."

Interviewer: "You haven't worked in years. What makes you think that your years as a housewife have prepared you for the work force demands of today?"

Response: "While I may not have earned a paycheck for my work, let me point out that during the past five years, I've developed a number of skills in the nonprofit sector that transfer to needs of your company. For example, I've directed four major fund-raising events, that required the same organizational and budget management skills this job requires. In addition, my efforts brought in contributions that consistently exceeded the organization's goals."

5.5 Getting the salary you deserve

The key to getting the salary you deserve is knowing the market value for your skills. (See Chapter 17 for a comprehensive approach to developing and quoting a salary range and Chapter 18 for responding to offers.) Women are usually their own worst enemies when quoting a salary or accepting an offer. Their biggest problem has been relying on the employer to be fair instead of taking responsibility themselves for getting the right salary. Key factors to remember are:

1. Employers are not going to take a protective or paternalistic attitude toward you and automatically give you a good salary. They are focused on being profitable and

that means paying any employee the least amount they have to.

2. A lot of women go into the interview uninformed about the worth of their skills, sometimes projecting the attitude that they would just be grateful to get the job. Some women have even been so excited about the job, they've forgotten to ask about salary. Before starting your job search, you should know the market value for your skills in your geographic area, and be prepared to quote a salary range that reflects that information.

3. Don't be afraid to negotiate salary or ask for time to consider a job offer. The employer has made an ego-investment by saying he or she wants you, and that means you have some time to think about the offer and possibly some room for negotiation—because the employer does not want to be rejected.

4. Don't refrain from asking for what you deserve because your husband works and you don't need the money. If the money is not a big issue for you because of a working spouse, then negotiate for increased benefits as a way of securing fair compensation based on the market value of your skills.

5.6 Some good news...

There are indeed some positive changes already in the works for the female members of the work force. First, because their numbers are growing they are beginning to have a greater voice in directing change. More and more corporations are offering greater flexibility, initiating such innovations as flextime, job sharing and telecommuting programs. On-site day-care services are more common and even elder care for parents of workers is being addressed to some extent. The work place is becoming more family-friendly.

The new management approach that corporate America is more frequently adopting means more room for women. Joan, the human resource vice president for a mid-sized manufacturing company, is now included with the team that develops business strategies for the company. After the first few months, the other team members welcomed her input and she now receives the bonuses and appreciation awarded all the other company executives.

There is more flexibility in the corporate world these days. Lois's position as vice president of finance for a major oil company exemplifies that. Securing the top financial position in a male-dominated company was no easy feat and was given based on capability and after gathering experience through several relocations around the country.

Some fields traditionally off-limits to women are now encouraging women. Some fields, such as science and engineering, are actually screaming for women to fill their quotas. It is encouraging to see some of the visible role models of those fields, like the top seismologists who shared information with the public on some of the major earthquakes on the West Coast.

The important point is that strides have been made, largely as a result of the efforts of a few—and if all women reach for their full measure as a matter of habit, then the equity that results will create a more positive and effective business environment for everyone.

Resolutions

1. A smart woman must recognize the gender obstacles in her path and overcome them.

2. Success requires turning situations fraught with obstacles into opportunities to demonstrate your capabilities.

3. Learn to be comfortable about promoting yourself, talking about your accomplishments, taking credit for your successes and demanding the promotions and salary you deserve.

4. Leave personal data off your resume. While it is usually impossible to hide the fact that you're female, there's no point in making an issue of it. Leave off photos, marital status, physical descriptions or references to husband or children.

5. It's best to use a functional resume when you want to exclude irrelevant jobs, have job gaps, want to summarize a lot of experience or are concerned about age.

6. The best preparation for a good interview is practice. Plan to have several practice sessions with friends and professionals before that big interview.

7. Anticipate interview questions about your personal life and practice several appropriate responses to typical questions. Your responses should address the employer's real needs while keeping the interview focused on the job.

8. Always project the right image during the interview. Dress conservatively and maintain a professional attitude and positive behavior. Young women should strive

to look serious and mature; avoid trendy looking attire. Older women should strive for an updated, sophisticated look. The standard navy blue suit is always a wise choice.

9. At the interview, shake hands and acknowledge everyone you meet, including receptionists and assistants.

10. During the interview, take credit for your achievements.

11. Demonstrate you are committed to a career by showing you're focused toward accomplishing a goal. Be able to tell interviewers how your jobs (or responsibilities) have been building toward a career.

12. If an offer is made for a lesser job than the one for which you applied, first consider your alternatives, then offer a compromise that will allow you to meet the employer's needs and still achieve your goal.

13. Don't be afraid to negotiate the salary you deserve.

14. After you get the job you want, immediately develop a plan to get your next job. Get the education and seek out the experiences you'll need to move forward.

15. The corporate world is transforming and room is opening up for the smart women who accept there is no easy road to the top and know that attaining their goal will require planning, hard work and commitment.

A job-hopper's resume

Linda Peterson
1111 Rodeo Road
Los Angeles, CA 90011
(213) 555-3434

Summary

Administrative assistant with more than 10 years of experience handling demanding, high-volume tasks in business and nonprofit sector. Background in banking, insurance and engineering offices. Strengths include ability to work under pressure and meet tight deadlines, organization and motivating others. A committed employee who takes the initiative to get the job done. Computer literate.

Selected Accomplishments

- Supervised a group of 15 in handling high-volume processing function for a financial institution and always met tight deadlines.
- Coordinated the efforts of 45 volunteers in a fundraiser, which provided a computer laboratory for a secondary school.
- Initiated and implemented a community effort to provide a posthumous ceremony and substantial monetary award of appreciation to the family of a high school star athlete.
- Set up a new color-coded filing system for a sales office, which allowed the sales people to retrieve information three times faster.
- Provided administrative support to seven professionals for three months while co-worker was on personal leave.
- Taught self WordPerfect and was able to generate two large reports for an executive meeting.

Work Experience

Administrative Assistant, ABC Temporary Services
Teller, Bank of America
Customer Service Representative, XSP Financial Services
Administrative Assistant, Carter Engineering Company

Education

Franklin Junior College—18 months toward AA in Business

Associations

President, Franklin School PTA
Officer of Franklin County Neighborhood Watch Program
Member of Toastmasters International

Return to the work force

MARIA SMITH
456 Parklane Avenue
Los Angeles, CA 90001
(213) 555-6650

SUMMARY

Self-motivated manager with more than 10 years of experience handling loss recovery and customer service responsibilities in a fast-paced office environment. Skilled in client relations, problem-solving and administration. Proficient at assessing priorities and delegating responsibilities. Able to generate a high energy level, which motivates employees. A diplomatic and determined professional who knows how to get the job done. PC literate.

SELECTED ACCOMPLISHMENTS

♦ Received a bonus for establishing a loss-recovery/customer-service department including development and implementation of policy, procedures manual and collection letters.

♦ Reduced collection delinquency from 35 percent to 10 percent within six months.

♦ Received a bonus for collecting 45 percent of the chargebacks within a year for a financial services group.

♦ Implemented a forbearance program for delinquent buyers, which improved customer relations, kept accounts from foreclosure and maintained receivables.

PROFESSIONAL HISTORY

Loss Recovery/Customer Service Manager

Vacation Industries, Inc.   6 ½ years

Managed a department of 14 people providing collections and customer service support for a million-dollar organization.

♦ Developed and implemented a collection and customer service process which included a manual, collection letters and administrative procedures.

♦ Implemented payment arrangement guidelines.

♦ Conducted training classes to develop skills in collection techniques.

♦ Tracked bankruptcy proceedings and worked with attorneys/court trustees on payment arrangements/proof of claims/final disposition.

♦ Set up lines of credit.

(continued)

Maria Smith, page 2

Assistant Collections Manager

A.B.C. Financial Services   2 ½ years

Handled real estate loans, foreclosures and setting up dealer accounts.

- ◆ Processed and approved loans.
- ◆ Handled collections, small claims and bankruptcy accounts.
- ◆ Handled account 60-90 days delinquent/120 days/chargeoffs.
- ◆ Ran TRW credit reports for loan approvals.

Loss Recovery/Customer Services Manager

National Service Center Tour & Travel Inc.   3 years

Managed Collections/Customer Service Department for a check-cashing/mailbox service for five locations.

- ◆ Implemented collections/customer service procedures.
- ◆ Supervised collections on return checks/skiptracing.
- ◆ Set up Western Union transactions.

Assistant Collections/Customer Service Manager for
        Commercial Accounts

PPP Systems (Division of MACON)   3 years

Managed the following clients: Southern California Utilities, Giant Aircraft, Blue Diamond International, Solid Manufacturing.

- ◆ Assisted customer service/collections manager with collection reports/sales reports.
- ◆ Employee phone monitoring 10 collectors and 14 customer service representatives.
- ◆ Handled client complaints.
- ◆ Set up lines of credit.
- ◆ Inventory control.

EDUCATION

California State University—Northridge
Major: Business Administration, Minor: Communication

Chapter 6

I'm too old

Sadly, the work force can often be an environment where the wisdom of experience is not valued as highly as other factors. Employers may be reluctant to hire older adults for a number of reasons: fear of failing health or limited stamina, concerns about whether they can afford to pay an individual with so many years of experience and doubts about the older worker's ability to integrate with a younger work force. While there are plenty of employers who do value the maturity and skills that seasoned employees bring to the job arena, it's wise for the older job seeker to play down age and focus on the accomplishments and positive energy that they have to offer.

6.1 Leave age off the resume

Alice had been looking for a secretarial job for more than six months and had sent out many standard chronological resumes and cover letters in response to newspaper ads. She had not received one call for an interview.

One day after hearing her frustration about the situation, her friend Stella asked to look at her resume. "Well, no wonder they're not calling you for an interview. They're probably throwing out your resume because they think you're too old. According to your resume, you have 33 years of experience. You need to change your resume."

Stella's situation had been similar. At the age of 60 when she looked for a marketing management position, she discovered her impressive resume wasn't opening the doors she thought it would. "I guess they thought I was so old that I might drop dead on the job," she said with a chuckle. "So I stopped advertising my age, and I got lots of interviews. Once the employers met me in person, I was able to connect with them, and my experience spoke for itself."

Resumes are not application forms

When preparing their resumes, some people still insist on accounting for all their adult time since high school, even when that style points out negative factors that could eliminate them from consideration. They are afraid they will not be considered if they don't use a standard chronological format.

But a resume is not a confession. While you should *never* lie or mislead with the material on your resume, you're under no obligation to provide information that could be used against you. Just as you would never include details about why you were fired from a previous job (or even that you were fired), you shouldn't construct your resume in such a way that it draws attention to your age, if it's not a plus.

If you're like many with perhaps three decades or more of work experience, it's likely that your early jobs were not as important to your career development as later jobs. For example, you may have started out working as a secretary, which led to your involvement in advertising. While you've spent the last 15 years as an account executive for two or three agencies, increasing the size and importance of your accounts, the first 15 years of experience as a secretary don't add a lot to your value. It might be best to just drop that experience from your resume.

Or consider using a functional resume format rather than the traditional chronological format, which involves listing your job experience from the most recent to your first and draws attention to the amount of time you've been working. The functional style allows for grouping experience by skill, which allows you to feature your strengths.

Eliminate dates

In addition, the functional resume format allows you to drop dates from your resume, or at least draw attention away from them. You can, for example, show an approximate number for years of experience and eliminate all dates, or indicate the number of years you worked at a company. (See resume examples in Chapter 5.)

What about the education section of your resume? Well, you're in luck if you returned to college as an adult, or earned a post-graduate degree later in your career. By all means, if you finally completed your MBA five years ago, list the date. (Of course, you don't need to mention you started it 15 years ago.)

But how can you avoid giving away your age when you received your degree in 1955? Many resume-writing books will tell you it's a *must* to include the year in which you graduated. They'll warn you that employers will suspect you're trying to hide something if you leave this off. While there is no guarantee that won't happen, if you have crafted a resume that showcases your skills and accomplishments in a way that makes it clear to prospective employers that you're an asset, then the employer isn't likely to toss your resume just because you left the dates off the education section.

Also, make note of this: At your age, you shouldn't be including any detail about your high school education. (You should have dropped this by the time you'd worked for 10 years.)

6.2 Making your "old" resume youthful

The example on pages 84-86 is Barbara's original resume, which makes it easy to determine that her age is probably over 50. In contrast, the resume on page 87 eliminates age as an issue and turns the resume into a more powerful selling tool. It has the following advantages:

- Dates are eliminated, bypassing negative stereotypes about age. Experience is sufficiently established with the reference to years in the summary statement. Since the resume is an advertising tool and not an application form, it is perfectly all right to leave dates off.
- A summary statement is added, which makes it convenient and easy for the prospective employer to quickly determine Barbara's qualifications without having to read the whole resume first. The personal information conveys energy.

Accomplishments are grouped together in one section, which gives them a greater positive impact than spreading them throughout the resume. This functional style eliminates the need to repeat similar information from job to job and allows for a shorter version of the resume.

6.3 Overcome age objections during the interview

By rewriting your resume, you may overcome the challenge of employers who object to hiring older workers. The next step, then, is to overcome their concerns during the interview. Your challenge at this point is to convince your interviewer, who may have preconceived ideas that older workers are inflexible or hard to train, that you are the ideal candidate and that you'll bring experience and enthusiasm to your job. This is your chance to take advantage of personal chemistry and to create a positive, strong and "youthful" image.

Barbara's "old" resume

Barbara Lopez
7344 Meridian Way
Los Angeles, CA
Home: 303-555-7900
Work: 303-555-3884

Work Experience

Southwest Company
Systems Analyst (October 1990-August 1994)

Provide primary Macintosh support for Southwest Corporate, including system setup and integration, application support and training. Knowledge of all aspects of desktop computing applications, operating systems and local area networks. Provide general support and training to company's senior executives and staffs in the use of Macintosh workstation and applications and access to external databases via Bridge, Dow Jones and Reuters. Implemented technology upgrade for the Santa Barbara Executive Conference Center, including remote communications with headquarters offices.

Accomplishments
- Implemented and upgraded all (350) of Corporate's Macintosh computers with current operating system software.
- Maintained all machines on current application software, mail and virus protection programs.

Systems Analyst (August 1988-October 1990)

Provided primary Macintosh support for Southwest Investment Management Company (SIMCO). Implemented and set up Macintosh workstations, including all hardware components, system and application software and network connections. Supported senior executives with Bridge and Reuters databases. Supported all Macintosh users and performed first-line troubleshooting.

Accomplishments
- Successfully relocated SIMCO's computers to a new location.
- Responsible for all network connections, all cable connects and completion of relocation schedule.

(continued)

Computer Operations Supervisor (March 1987-August 1988)

Supervised the Southwest Corporate computing facility. Maintained multiple minicomputers, local area networks, host attached printers and a communication control center. Coordinated Corporate Units computer operations support, interface with clients, vendors, management and staff. Performed personnel selections and evaluation. Determined training requirements and provided much of the training for subordinates. Developed plans and schedules for 24-hour staffing of computer operations facility. Made technical and financial decisions.

Accomplishments

• Supervised relocation of multiple computing facilities, including planning, staffing, training, execution and troubleshooting.
• Received departmental award for outstanding service, related to the Southwest Restack Project.

Lead Computer Operator (February 1984-February 1987)

Supervised a staff of seven. Ensured adequate staffing and scheduling to meet production requirements. Supervised the operation and maintenance of multiple computerized systems in support of corporate unit organizations. Interfaced with operating company data centers. Led development of system maintenance, backup, recovery and diagnostic routines. Performed training and troubleshooting for computer users and operators. Responsible for all hardware connections and wiring requirements for Southwest Headquarters.

Accomplishments

• Oversaw implementation of new multiple systems, including Four-Phase Series IV/95, Hewlett Packard 3000/68, Xerox Distributed Office Systems Network (Ethernet) and Network Communication Center.
• Trained staff to operate and maintain systems, including troubleshooting functions and client consultation.

Computer Operator (August 1972-February 1984)

Operated Corporate Systems' Data 100 Remote Terminal. Provided keypunch service and report distribution. Maintained job logs and prepared project completion reports.

(continued)

Barbara Lopez
page 3

Keypunch Operator (June 1965-July 1971)
Provided backup for Lead Operator. Trained new employees on credit card and wholesale data entry. Performed keypunch functions.

Technical Environments Experience
- Macintosh computers: All models (350 workstations)
- Four-Phase Series IV/95 minicomputer (four processors, 90 workstations)
- Hewlett Packard 3000/68 (40 workstations)
- Xerox Distributed Office Systems local Network (300 workstations, multiple servers)
- 3-Com local network (400 workstations)

Education
Bachelor of Science, Organizational Behavior 1964
University of San Francisco

Associate In Arts, 1960
East Los Angeles College

Business Data Processing Certificate Program, 1967
East Los Angeles College

Personal Data
Languages: Bilingual in English and Spanish
Leisure Activities: Snow skiing, running, tennis, community service projects, classical music.

Barbara's "youthful" resume

BARBARA LOPEZ
7344 Meridian Way
Los Angeles, CA
303-555-7900

SUMMARY

Over 15 years of progressive experience providing system support for Southwest Company. Skilled in setup and integration, application support, troubleshooting, staffing, training and supervision. Technical environments experience includes all Macintosh models, Four-Phase Series IV/95 minicomputer, Hewlett Packard 3000/68, Xerox Distributed Office Systems Local Network and 3-Com local network. Fluent in Spanish.

ACCOMPLISHMENTS

♦ Implemented and upgraded all of Southwest's Corporate Division Macintosh computers (350) with current operating system software. Maintained all machines on current application software, mail and virus protection programs.

♦ Successfully relocated, on schedule, all the computers for the Investment Management Company (SIMCO) to a new location. Responsible for all network and cable connections.

♦ Supervised relocation of multiple computing facilities, including planning, staffing, training, execution and troubleshooting. Received departmental award for outstanding service.

♦ Oversaw implementation of new multiple systems, including Four-Phase Series IV/95, Hewlett Packard 3000/68, Xerox Distributed Office Systems Network (Ethernet) and Network Communication Center.

♦ Trained several staffs to operate and maintain systems, including troubleshooting functions and client consultation.

♦ Started up a corporate systems computer terminal facility. Opened with one RJE station and added DATA 100, IBM 3777 remote station and a four-phase system.

CAREER PROGRESSION

Southwest Company, Los Angeles, Calif.

♦ Systems Analyst, Corporate Divisions
♦ Systems Analyst, Investment Management Co.
♦ Supervisor, Computer Operations
♦ Lead Computer Operator
♦ Computer Operator

EDUCATION

B.S., Organizational Behavior, University of San Francisco
A.A., Los Angeles College
Business Data Processing Certificate Program, L.A. College

You'll want to start by making a powerful first impression and to do as much in that moment to avoid reinforcing any negative stereotypes the interviewer may have about older employees. You have about 25 additional seconds after the prospective employer meets you to confirm or change the impression you make in the first five seconds.

You can ace the interview with:

- A polished appearance. Do whatever it takes. Replace the bifocals with contact lenses. Women should be sure their hairstyle is flattering and makeup is moderate and contemporary. (A makeup consultant at a department store can help you put together an updated look. And it's free.) Men should have a stylish haircut. Also, avoid too much perfume or cologne. In fact, it's best to go without.

- A "with-it" wardrobe. Wear a new suit and shoes that are modern. A sales clerk at a nice department store can help you put together one or two attractive ensembles.

- A "team" attitude. Don't act like your interviewer's parent, and chances are you'll be perceived as a contemporary, even if there is a significant age difference. Start off by referring to the interviewer as "dear" or "son," and you'll only draw attention to the gap. Avoid condescending comments such as, "When I was your age..."

- Research. Try to find out about the company's philosophy and culture through your network or by observations beforehand. If the company emphasizes tradition and stability, you'll be able to present yourself as a dependable and experienced addition to the team. If change and energy seem to color the company, you'll want to be sure and appear as a flexible and enthusiastic candidate.

During the interview, it's important to relate to the interviewer, whatever age, as a contemporary. Perhaps you've never worked with—or *for*—someone so young, and you may have concerns about this. But you don't want this to come across in the interview. Approach everyone with optimism and enthusiasm, and it's likely you'll experience less resistance.

If it's been awhile since you've gone through the interviewing process, be prepared for some changes. You may be surprised by some rather unorthodox questions, such as, "Please describe yourself in one word," "What do you hope people will say about you when you're gone?" or "If you were a tree, what kind of tree would you be?" Be positive, have fun with it, but by all means take the process seriously.

Oh, and one important piece of advice: Don't ask about pension plans or retirement benefits during your initial interview.

6.4   Be prepared to handle challenging questions

If you suspect your interviewer is bothered by your age, be careful when responding to his or her questions. If you hear statements such as, "We go through a lot of change around here," and "Our employees are expected to be flexible," you must respond to the unspoken concern here. You might answer by saying something like, "In my previous job, we experienced constant upheaval as we went through numerous organizations. I attribute my longevity with the company and my ability to advance despite the turmoil to my ability to adapt to change and initiate new ways to achieve the company's goals."

If your interviewer seems concerned about your being overqualified, stress how you see each new situation as an opportunity to learn and grow. If he or she seems concerned about your motivational level, find a way to mention some of the high-energy activities you have been involved with on or off the job.

Not often, but every once in awhile, an interviewer may ask outright about your age. While you may, rightfully, feel offended, it certainly won't help if you react indignantly. Instead, respond to the employer's concern. You might say something like, "If you're concerned that I might be too 'set in my ways' to adapt to a new environment, let me assure you that I welcome change. Even though I spent the last 10 years in the same company, I held a variety of positions, learned a number of new skills and worked with and for many people. In fact, new challenges motivate me and it's one of the reasons I'm so intrigued by this position with your company."

Over the years, you've gathered a wealth of experience and skills. And hopefully, the workplace is learning to appreciate the wisdom and accomplishments of its older employees. But clearly, those more "seasoned" workers do face challenges in landing jobs that younger employees don't. Challenges, however, can certainly be turned into opportunities with just a little work.

Resolutions

1. Play down your age on your resume as much as possible.

2. Consider restructuring your resume, using the functional format rather than the chronological format.

3. In the education section of your resume, leave off the dates if your degrees were earned more than 20 years ago.

4. For a job interview, be sure your appearance and clothing are contemporary so that your image is youthful.

5. Research the company prior to your interview, to determine the corporate "image." Is it youthful? Conservative? Then respond accordingly.

6. During the interview, don't draw attention to age gaps with the interviewer by making remarks such as, "When I was your age..."

7. Maintain a positive attitude, even if you do have concerns about the youth of your interviewer or are surprised by some unorthodox interviewing techniques.

8. Respond to challenging questions such as, "Can you adapt to change?" by exhibiting enthusiasm and pointing out recent achievements that reflect your abilities, and you'll be sure to ease the interviewer's concerns.

Chapter 7

I'm too young

It's a Catch-22. You're young and anxious to get started on the road to a productive career—but you can't get a good job because you don't have experience! You confront employers who don't seem impressed by your educational credentials or your eagerness and seem to, instead, focus on your lack of paid work history. They may even express doubts about your maturity, dependability and commitment. You counter, however, "How can I prove my commitment if no one will give me a chance?"

Well, let me assure you that even in this age of downsizings, reorganizations and demands for corporate accountability, there are ways to get yourself on the road to a successful career. And believe it or not, it's not your *youth* that employers object to as much as it is your inexperience. In fact, your youth can be a real advantage to employers who have had to cut their hiring budgets to entry-level wages and who must demand flexibility, overtime hours and the energy it often takes to keep short-staffed departments going. And as long as you can overcome the objections, you'll find that you can indeed jump-start your career. Here's how:

7.1 Turn extracurricular activities into job applicable experiences

The tall young man in the pinstriped suit moved purposefully among the attendees of the International Toastmaster's Conference, directing others and generally performing his duties as one of the district leaders. David's springy step, energetic attitude and trim figure were the stamp of a surfer. Yet, on this Saturday afternoon, when most of his friends were at the beach enjoying the California sun, he was assisting speakers and mingling with professionals twice his age.

His friends had tried to coax him into joining them, but he insisted it was necessary to postpone some of the fun activities to lay a solid foundation for his future. Even during his college years, he eagerly took advantage of internships and volunteer experiences to add to his professional experiences. These efforts helped land him his first job with a solid career track.

He got the interview for his job through a networking contact while involved in community fundraisers. The interviewer had been impressed with his resume, which detailed the types of skills he was looking for to fill the position. However, David had not acquired these skills through any paid work experience. But instead he presented his volunteer activities—with the chamber of commerce, an *ad hoc* committee to the school board, Toastmasters and a program to provide meals to the elderly—as career experience. The interviewer felt that the skills David had gathered through his involvements were a perfect match for the open position. In addition, he thought David's involvement reflected a mature attitude. He also commented that holding a job all during his college years showed he was a disciplined, hard worker.

While some employers have a negative bias against those under 25 because they feel they are lacking in maturity and have a poor work ethic, you can disprove their perception by demonstrating your involvement in professional activities requiring leadership and personal commitment.

Involving yourself in worthwhile activities as soon as feasible as a young adult (you can even start while in high school) builds character, develops skills that can transfer to a job and provides networking contacts and experiences that can be drawn on to develop that first resume.

Join community groups, professional associations and other organizations where people have the same interests. And become active! Volunteer to put together the organizational newsletter or help plan that special event. This experience can translate on your resume to communications, organization, management and leadership skills. To get started, check the *Encyclopedia of Associations* for a listing of professional organizations that you might join. (See Section 21.1.)

7.2 A resume with the impact of 10 years' experience

The resume on page 94 is an effective advertising tool that shows David's full range of skill and experience. It reflects his technical capability and shows, through his volunteer efforts, that he has social skills. When you have less than five years of experience, it is helpful to add relevant extracurricular activities that will enhance your resume. Its best to use the functional resume style shown when combining extracurricular activities with job experience.

7.3   Network your way into job opportunities

When Chad started frequenting a country western club, little did he imagine that it would lead him to his first "real" job. As a frequently unemployed musician, Chad often went to the club to play pool or meet with friends. Through some of the bar's "regulars," he was introduced to Thomas, a general manager of a testing laboratory.

Chad rarely expressed his career dreams or desire to grow into a more traditional work environment. He worked to develop a friendly rapport with everyone in the group. He was quite popular, dispensing witticisms, being playful and generally displaying a personality that said he liked being loose and unstructured in his approach.

One night Thomas approached him about an opening at his company. He told Chad that he knew he would fit in because he had a personality similar to the other people at the laboratory. He told him that the supervisor would train him for a position. After that, he told Chad he didn't want to talk about the job anymore—he disliked talking about work when he was off.

Chad got a job at the laboratory the next week and was trained on the job to handle the responsibilities. It was the same laboratory that had rejected his application two months earlier when he had applied on his own.

Looking for a good fit

Employers not only look for skilled, motivated workers, they seek individuals who will fit in with the rest of the workers, whose personalities reflect that of the company. Networking with people you get along with is likely to lead to introductions to others you'll also get along with—which can lead to job opportunities that are likely to be a good fit for you.

Once you have your career goal in mind, seize every opportunity to develop contacts that might lead you to information about work environments you want to pursue. Let others know of your availability and skills. You may establish these contacts through professional organizations or leisure activities—like Chad did. What's important is to get involved in the kinds of activities you enjoy and that you'll know others like you will be involved in.

David's "mature" resume

David Borne
75 Rockingham
Santa Monica, CA 10010
(312) 555-5001

Summary of Capabilities

Experienced in chemical plant operation including quality control and technical support. Strengths include abilities to analyze complex processes for improvements, lead and motivate others and organize and carry out demanding projects. A self-starter and hard-working professional with excellent communication and interpersonal skills.

Education

B.S. Chemistry, University of Wisconsin
Management Communications, University of California/Santa Barbara

Relevant Accomplishments

Cost Improvements
Part of a small engineering team that took old, poorly operating chemical production units back to high-rate operation, set new production records, met product requirements and exceeded profit forecasts.
Suggested a plan to reorganize the quality control function of a small fertilizer plant which reduced product quality complaints to zero.

Project Management
Recruited, trained and supervised more than 40 volunteers for a program that regularly delivers meals to the elderly.

Leadership
Was elected District One Manager for the largest Toastmasters unit in the Western Region six months after joining.
Volunteer for the Santa Monica Chamber of Commerce for two years.

Employment

Chemical Engineer II, United Chemical Company, 1989-Present
Support quality control laboratories of large and complex chemical plants. Assist in preparation of all analytical functions for plant startup.

Professional Associations and Organizations

Association of Chemical Professionals
Santa Monica Chamber of Commerce
Toastmasters International
Volunteer, "Meals on Wheels" for the elderly

7.4 Interviewing skills for the young job seeker

Whenever you talk about employment, the conversation should be considered an interview. Yet when it comes to the *real* interview, you should be especially prepared to sell yourself. All of your planning, resume preparation, letter-writing and pavement-pounding has led you to that meeting. Advance preparation is the best way to carry the interview off successfully. You'll need to:

Know yourself. Sections 1.4, 1.5 and 1.6 will provide guidelines for discovering your unique combination of talents and setting a career goal. As a newcomer to the work force, it's especially important that you have a thorough understanding of your skills and strengths, since you are likely to have less experience to demonstrate those strengths. Be prepared to identify what gives you satisfaction in a job. Be focused in response to questions about your goals, but make sure that when explaining them to the employer they dovetail with his or her department goals. The more thorough your self-assessment, the more comfortable you will be handling difficult or "surprise" questions.

Know the current market value for your skills. Salary requirements is one of the first issues a prospective employer is likely to ask about. It's likely that, as an entry-level candidate, your salary level may be lower than what a more experienced worker might draw. But be sure you've researched industry salaries thoroughly before the interview. Initially you may be able to put that question off by saying your requirements are open or negotiable depending on the job, but ultimately you should be prepared with a salary range that is appropriate for the job and your qualifications. (See Chapter 17.)

Know what the interviewer wants. Before the interview, tap into your network to gain important unpublished information you'll need—specifically the interviewer's management style, what traits he or she is looking for, the department problems and needs, and salary range for the position.

Analyze published information to determine how the company's goals, benefits and culture relates to your needs and objectives. Does the company offer a sound future? Would you invest in its stock? Do you know any of its employees? How do they like the company? What is the company's purpose and products? Who is the competition?

What benefits does the company offer such as insurance, savings plans, vacations, overtime pay, stock options? What are the future plans? (See Section 21.1.)

Interview skills: Practice makes perfect

Steve, 26, walked into his interview with a sales company to discover a three-person panel. They started the interview by asking him to tell them something about himself. After 10 minutes of nonstop discourse, they knew that he was recently divorced, had joint custody of his 5-year-old child who stayed with him on alternate weeks and that he had trouble keeping a decent housekeeper.

None of this, of course, had any relevance to the position. And his revelations merely caused the panel to worry that Steve might have family problems and financial burdens that would distract him from his work.

Julia was the next interview scheduled with the panel. Her response to the "tell us about yourself" question was a little different. She talked for only eight minutes, but she made no eye contact and looked at a side wall for most of that time. Finally one of the interviewers caught her eye and cut her response short.

Both those individuals blew their interview. The panel decided that Steve probably needed counseling and certainly Julia needed something for her nerves. Neither of these individuals was prepared.

If you have been networking and explaining your skills and abilities to a variety of people, you should be quite proficient at selling yourself by the time you get to that important interview. But in order to ensure a truly winning interview, you need to spend a lot more time preparing yourself. Consider the following:

- Work with a few close friends to conduct mock interviews with you. It would probably be a good idea to ask people who have knowledge of your skill area.

- Develop a list of questions you want to ask about the company. There's nothing that irks interviewers as much as a candidate who can't think of a question to ask. Or worse, a candidate who only asks about vacation time and benefits.

- Prepare in advance your "tell us about yourself" statement. Make it succinct, just two minutes or so, and focus on what's relevant to the employer. For example, if you're interviewing for a job as a fitness trainer, point out your involvement in college athletics, your achievements as a member of sports teams and your coaching of youth sports. Don't spend a lot of time talking about unrelated jobs. The important thing is to prepare thoroughly.

- Develop an interview kit or a portfolio, a scrapbook or collection of items that reflect your skills and experience. The kit can contain anything that will help demonstrate that you have performed meaningful work. Some typical items for inclusion are samples of your work, samples of reports, photos of equipment worked with and letters of commendation. You should always control the use of this kit. Present the kit, or elements of it, to the interviewer, but be sure it is returned to you.

- Bring a couple of extra copies of your resume and a completed application you can use to copy information onto the prospective company's application.

Project the right image

You have about 30 seconds after you meet the interviewer to make a positive first impression, so your appearance should solicit an immediate "thumbs up" attitude from the interviewer. You want the focus to be on your skills, so your appearance should not draw undue attention but should indicate confidence and an ability to fit in with the company's culture.

When in doubt (which you shouldn't be if you've done your homework and researched the corporate culture), always wear the uniform of business—a dark or neutral-colored business suit. Even if the company environment turns out to be quite casual, you'll communicate to your interviewer that you are professional and know the rules of the job-hunting game.

Arrive at least 15 minutes early to allow time to get your bearings and get a feel for the organization. Have the name and phone number of your contact. This is especially necessary if something happens along the way and you are unable to be on time. While waiting in the reception area, read the company literature and observe the interaction between employees. Try to pick out a topic for positive comment when you meet the interviewer. Under all circumstances, have a positive attitude.

7.5 Difficult questions that might come up

Interviewer: "Don't you think you are a little too young for this job?"

Response: "I realize that I am young, but I believe that the work I've done with volunteer activities—plus working while attending school full-time—reflects the behavior of a mature person. I believe that I will be able to fit in with your staff and am willing to work to establish myself and gain their respect as a contributing team member."

Interviewer: "Why do you want to work for us?"

Response: "I've done some reading about your company and was impressed with _____ , and I would like to be a part of making that goal a reality."

Interviewer: "What is your five-year goal?"

Response: "First of all, if I get this job, I would like to do well in it and grow with the department and company, taking on more responsibility when the opportunity presented itself. My long-term goal is to establish myself as a knowledgeable professional in my field."

Interviewer: "Why should I hire you when so many out there have so much more experience?"

Response: "Because what I believe I may be lacking in experience is balanced out by my enthusiasm, energy and fresh outlook, which may bring some new and profitable ideas to your team."

Interviewer: "What makes you think a young whippersnapper like you can fit in with this group and make a contribution?"

Response: "I agree that your group, as you outlined it, is impressive, but I've had an opportunity to prove myself successfully with other groups and was able to gain their respect and make a contribution. For instance, (give an example of such an accomplishment). I believe that, given the chance, I can do the same here."

Interviewer: "I'm afraid that I'd have to start you at a lower salary until you could come up to par in experience."

Response: "I can understand that you want to be assured that I'll be able to handle the responsibilities of the job. But, based on my research, the salary I'm requesting is competitive with what other companies like yours are paying for my experience. Plus, I believe I have already demonstrated some track record with my involvement with (volunteer activities, etc.) and those activities increased my skills. Based on the goals you've outlined for the department, I believe those skills will add immediate value to the organization. So I think the salary I'm requesting is equitable."

Resolutions

1. As early as you can, get involved in as many activities as possible that relate to your field. The skills gathered in these extracurricular activities will transfer to your job situations and beef up your resume.

2. Join professional organizations in your field and *get active!* Offer to write the newsletter or organize an event. Do anything that will give you more accomplishments and achievements to boost your value to potential employers.

3. For a list of organizations, check the *Encyclopedia of Associations* in the reference section of the library.

4. If you've had nonpaid experience in which you've gathered some skills and achievements that apply toward your career, play them up in your resume. Treat them as you would work experience.

5. Consider a functional resume format, so that you can best highlight your transferable skills and downplay your negligible work history.

6. Start building your network as soon as possible. Identify those avenues in which you can meet people with like interests and career goals, and make every effort to establish relationships with individuals who may provide you with information, advice, job leads, support and more.

7. Be aware that employers not only want to hire skilled workers, they're also looking for individuals who "fit in," whose personalities and work styles match those of the other workers in the company. As you seek out job opportunities, keep this in mind.

8. Know the current market value for your skills. Be sure you're looking at resources that reflect your level of expertise as well as the regional area in which you live.

9. Practice, practice, practice for your job interview. Set up role-playing sessions with friends.

10. Memorize a brief, three-minute speech that tells an interviewer the most pertinent points about *you*. Be sure

to leave out personal information, irrelevant detail and anything that could be perceived as negative.

11. Make sure your appearance for an interview is appropriate. You want to look mature, confident and professional. When in doubt, stick to the dark business suit, and go for a conservative look.

12. Prepare yourself for potential "difficult" questions during an interview. You may be challenged by your interviewer that you're too young or inexperienced. Prepare some answers.

Chapter 8

I'm a minority

The law does not limit its protection against discrimination in employment to "minorities" but rather covers "protected classes." Title VII of the Civil Rights Act of 1964, as amended by the Equal Employment Opportunity Act of 1972 and the Civil Rights Act of 1991, is the major federal law prohibiting discrimination in employment on the basis of race, color, religion, sex or national origin. The Age Discrimination in Employment Act of 1967, as amended protects applicants and employees 40 years of age or older from discrimination, and the Equal Pay Act of 1963, as amended, prohibits sex discrimination in payment of wages to women and men performing substantially equal work in the same establishment. Title VII is administered by the Equal Employment Opportunity Commission (EEOC) and the courts. In addition, there are many federal laws that enforce the rights of specific groups, and some states' Fair Employment laws expressly address certain types of preemployment issues.

Even with federal and state laws, it is a fact that job discrimination still exists—though it's sometimes difficult to identify. How can you prove that your resume may have been put aside because of a street address that indicates a "wrong side" of town, or a last name that implies you're of a certain ethnic group, or a first name that implies the wrong gender? You can't. The best defense is to recognize that discrimination might exist—don't focus on gender or race in your resume, and do focus on your professionalism and achievements.

8.1 Focus on skills and achievements, not ethnicity, in your resume

Employers want competent, confident workers for their jobs and that is what Joe conveyed about himself in his resume.

Joe, a Black marketing professional, started an immediate job search after his company gave a two-month notice of a planned reduction. Instead of relying just on advertised positions, he started his search at the public library. (See Section 21.1.) He researched the needs of 50 companies he thought could use his skills. He called each company to get the name and title of the executive in charge of marketing. He then sent a letter targeted to the needs of each company, plus a three-page resume.

His associates laughed at his resume and asked if he was trying to write a book. He took the teasing good-naturedly and persisted with his plan. His resumes were detailed because he was concerned about his lack of a degree and wanted to convey his capabilities well. Nowhere in Joe's resume, however, did he indicate any personal information or any affiliation that might have revealed his race. While Joe was proud to be Black, as indicated by his involvement in a number of community organizations and ethnic causes, he knew that, despite laws against minority discrimination, a photo or a mention of his work with the organization 100 Black Men might cause a resume screener or prospective employer to eliminate his resume from the running.

His method worked. Within three weeks he had five interviews in response to the resumes and ultimately landed a position two weeks before the final layoff was announced by his company.

Because companies ultimately want the best person for their positions, it is to your advantage to make a strong presentation of your qualifications with your first approach to the company. Any reference to gender or ethnicity as part of this approach might dilute your chances for consideration. Review your resume carefully, and have two other people review it, in order to weed out those types of references. Remember, your objective with the resume is only to get to the interview. Hopefully, chemistry will then take over.

8.2   What the interviewer can't ask

The EEOC regards with "extreme disfavor" inquiries concerning race, color (skin, eyes, hair, etc.), religion, sex, national origin, ancestry, marital status and physical or mental disabilities. Questions that serve no lawful purpose are based on factors that do not bear a demonstrable relationship to an applicant's ability or qualification as an employee. For example:

> *What is your race?*
>
> *Native language?*
>
> *What country are you from?*
>
> *What country are your parents from?*

What kind of last name is that?

Are you from Africa or the Caribbean?

A standard response to any illegal question(s) about race should refer back to the job. For example:

Are you concerned that my race might have some bearing on the job?

May I ask how race bears on my ability to do the job?

Wait for the interviewer to relate the question back to the job. If it cannot be done or the person states they were just "curious," then ignore the question. Sometimes an interviewer might slip and ask a question out of spontaneous curiosity. But one of the suggested responses should serve to put the person back on track. If it does not, you probably should indicate that race or whatever the characteristic being inquired about seems to be a negative factor preventing you from consideration, and terminate the interview.

8.3 What the interviewer might ask that may be legal—but may signal prejudice

Federal law does not expressly prohibit inquiries concerning an applicant's race, color, religion, sex, national origin or physical or mental disabilities. However, such inquiries must directly relate to a Bona Fide Occupational Qualification (BFOQ). If any of the job qualifications or selection standards have the effect of screening out minority groups, even when unintentional, the employer must be able to prove that: (1) the standards are significantly related to job performance, (2) the standards are required by business necessity, and (3) no alternate nondiscriminatory standards can be developed to meet the requirements of the job.

Here are a few examples of legally asked questions and appropriate responses:

Interviewer: "Do you think you'd have a problem working with a predominantly white staff?"

Response: "I am comfortable that I will be able to fit in and successfully handle the job. I've worked successfully in the past as part of an all-white team." (Be able to provide examples.)

Inquiries concerning an applicant's race must directly relate to a BFOQ, and the employer must be sure that any qualifications imposed are significantly related to successful job performance.

Interviewer: "Would you have to take off for any religious holidays?"

Response: "Do the work demands prohibit any time off?"

Questions relating to availability to work on Saturdays, Sundays or holidays are not automatically considered violations if all applicants are asked. But such inquiries should not be made when business necessity or job-relatedness cannot be proven.

Interviewer: "What language do you speak at home?"

Response: "Are there language requirements for the job?"

Inquiries may be made into the applicant's ability to read, write and speak English or foreign languages when required for a specific job. But questions about the applicant's lineage, ancestry, national origin, descent, place of birth, mother tongue, nationality of applicant's parents or spouse, or how the applicant acquired the ability to read, write or speak a foreign language are all inappropriate.

Chances are, your minority status is evident to your interviewer. But you still may be asked questions that attempt to confirm your race or ethnic group—or questions that communicate the interviewer's concern with your status. When confronted with this situation, it helps to understand that, in most cases, such questions reflect not an extreme bigotry but rather a concern that you'll "fit in." In addition to finding an employee who has the skills and experience to do the job, employers cite "fit" as one of the most important qualities they look for in a candidate. And, in most cases, "fit" translates to "being like me." Thus, if you're "different" than your employer, your ability to fit in with the group may be suspect.

When responding to questions regarding your ethnic status, keep in mind that you want to resolve the interviewer's fears that you'll be a comfortable fit.

8.4   You don't get the job—what can you do?

Yolanda, a Hispanic woman, wanted a management career in entertainment and was willing to start at the bottom and work her way up.

She brought 10 years of varied administrative experience to the industry, including five years with major studios and three with large companies in two other industries. She believed she was more than qualified for the administrative assistant position she heard about at one of the studios. So she pursued the opportunity with excitement.

After obtaining the name of the personnel representative through one of her networking contacts, she carefully prepared a resume making sure that she showed pertinent experience for each requirement that had been specified. She had her resume reviewed by a career counselor before submitting it to make sure there was no information that would cause it to be eliminated from consideration. Because her surname was not Hispanic, there was no indication of her ethnicity. She mailed her resume and was pleasantly surprised when called for an interview. She was told on the phone that her resume had been selected along with five others, out of a pool of more than 100 who had applied.

While she was waiting in the studio's reception area for her turn to speak with the personnel representative, she talked with a White applicant who was also applying for the position. After learning the other woman's background, Yolanda felt satisfied that she was more qualified for the position and believed she surely would be referred to the manager for interview.

She was wrong. The other applicant was referred to the manager for further consideration, and Yolanda was told they would call her if something came up. At first, she was upset, feeling that she had been discriminated against. Then she shrugged her shoulders, smiled and said, "Oh well, there's a better opportunity coming for me."

While you may suspect an interviewer was prejudiced, more than likely you can't prove you were the most qualified out of all the candidates but weren't hired because of discrimination.

But if you believe you were actually discriminated against, then you might want to pursue a case. Any interaction you have with the employer has potential EEO implications, even before the interview—for example, comments or questions made when you are greeted in the waiting area. Questions or comments like the ones listed below, no matter how casually posed, may be evidence of a pattern of discrimination and thereby adequate cause for instigating a suit:

> *Are you single, married or divorced?*
>
> *Would you like to be called Miss, Ms. or Mrs.?*
>
> *Do you plan to have a family?*
>
> *Have you ever been arrested?*
>
> *What was your maiden name?*
>
> *What is the nationality of your parents?*
>
> *Are there any holidays other than those usually observed that would require you to be absent?*

Where were you born?

Of what country are you a citizen?

What is your native language?

Who should we notify in case of an emergency?

What clubs, societies or organizations do you belong to?

What kind of discharge did you receive from the military?

Do you have any disability?

Can you read well enough to take the test?

8.5   What to do if you believe you have a discrimination case

There have been important class action, as well as individual, suits brought against companies for noncompliance. In instances where employees have won, large monetary awards have been granted and the hiring policies of the defending companies completely changed. Frequently, these cases uncover unfair hiring patterns throughout a company; in other cases, a single interviewer may have been careless about what he or she said or wrote down.

Costs and fees notwithstanding, employers are usually willing to fight suits until they can no longer prevail. So, before instigating a suit, be sure you have documented all of the facts surrounding your case, and be prepared for the process to take a long time (usually years). But even a long uphill battle is worth the positive change that can be made in the fight against discrimination, so if you believe that you have been discriminated against under the law, you should immediately contact:

The U.S. Equal Employment Opportunity Commission
2401 E Street, NW
Washington, DC 20507

Or call 800-USA-EEOC to contact an EEOC field office (for the hearing impaired, EEOC's TDD number is 202-634-7057).

It's a sad fact that discrimination does exist. But, for that matter, discrimination exists for reasons other than race or cultural background. (How's this for absurd? One resume screener rejected a candidate because he graduated from a university that beat the screener's school in basketball!) The best way to counter it is to downplay—don't apologize for—those characteristics that may differentiate you from your prospective employer. And put the focus on your accomplishments and job skills—in your resume, on your application and in your interviews.

Resolutions

1. Your goal in submitting a resume should be to avoid the deselection process and prompt a call for an interview. Avoid references to affiliations (NAACP, Jewish Defense League, Hispanic Alliance)—unless those references are considered positives for landing the job.

2. Do not send a photo with your resume. (This is almost always considered inappropriate.)

3. Since some surnames make ethnicity obvious, some people have opted to change their name so it will not be an impediment to their career. If you decide to make a change, it should be done legally and not just to apply for a job.

4. Being the most qualified candidate, no matter what your race, does not automatically guarantee you a position. In addition to skills, employers look at motivational level, personality and ability to "fit" with the company.

5. Don't always be quick to assume that you are being discriminated against because you were not the successful candidate for a position. That attitude is self-defeating, lessens your confidence and may inhibit you from pursuing other opportunities that are right around the corner. If you continue to be rejected by employers for the same kind of position, get some feedback on your qualifications, presentation and strategy from professionals in your field of interest. You may need to apply for a different level of position, enhance your qualifications or use a different strategy for approaching that market (see Chapter 20).

6. Sometimes you'll have all the tickets and lose out to someone less qualified because the person making the decision liked the other person better. It happens—and one day it will happen for you. So, if you don't succeed in getting one position, for whatever the reason, don't be discouraged.

7. After you have presented yourself in a professional manner, demonstrating that you would fit in the organization, and you sense a lack of interest because of your ethnicity, there is nothing else that you can do and qualifications won't make a difference—so move on.

Chapter 9

I have a disability

Everyone needs to have the freedom and confidence to be productive members of society. Unfortunately misconceptions and negative stereotypes about people with disabilities have prevented some from being readily accepted into the mainstream work force. Usually the discrimination is levied against people with visible disabilities, but often those people with "unseen" disabilities can end up experiencing discrimination as well.

The Americans With Disabilities Act covers more than obvious disabilities like hearing or vision impairments or wheelchair users. The law extends to those with hidden disabilities like diabetes, cancer and mental illnesses. The law protects some 43 million disabled Americans. While it is helping to open doors of opportunity by taking the spotlight off disabilities and focusing on abilities, discrimination may still be a challenge.

9.1 Americans with Disabilities Act (ADA): The basic points

ADA is designed to halt discrimination against individuals with disabilities in employment, public accommodations, transportation, state and local government services and telecommunications.

Under the employment provisions of ADA, a company may not discriminate against a qualified person with a disability with regard to: job application procedures; hiring, advancement or discharge of employees; and compensation, job training and/or other terms of employment. In addition, a company must make reasonable accommodations to the known physical or mental limitations of qualified applicants or employees with disabilities.

But the law does not require a company to hire or promote people who are not qualified just because they have disabilities. It is designed to provide equal opportunity in the workplace for qualified people with disabilities.

The important points of the law translate as follows:

1. Individuals protected under ADA include individuals recovering from drug and alcohol abuse, people with emotional disturbances and mental illnesses, those who are HIV positive, people with cancer and people with physical scars, as well as wheelchair users and those with hearing or vision impairments. Family members of those with disabilities also are covered.

2. Probably the single most important right afforded to persons with disabilities under the new law is the right to "reasonable accommodation." In general, reasonable accommodation is defined as any change in the work environment or in the way things are customarily done to allow an individual with a disability an equal employment opportunity. Examples of reasonable accommodation include: making existing facilities wheelchair-accessible; restructuring jobs, modifying work schedules and reassigning employees to vacant positions; acquiring devices or modifying equipment, examinations, training materials or policies. The law states that if the person is otherwise qualified to perform the essential functions of the job, he or she cannot be discriminated against just because an accommodation must be made.

3. A person with a disability is not required to reveal that information to the employer in person, on applications or resumes. If he or she voluntarily reveals the disability, the prospective employer is legally required to treat this information as strictly confidential. Notes should not be made on the application or interview record concerning the individual's medical condition.

4. A person with a disability has a right to expect fair and equitable treatment in an interview. Most employers are aware of the necessity of being consistent in their approach when questioning all candidates. They know to ask questions about an individual's ability to perform the essential duties and functions of the job and not refer to the disability. Also, the ADA requires that employers pay the same salary to employees with disabilities and employees without disabilities who perform the same essential functions. Essential functions are tasks that are fundamental to the job. For example:

   • Driving is an essential function of a truck driver.
   • Typing is an essential function of a word processor.

- Answering the phone is an essential function of a receptionist.
- Travel is an essential function of many salespeople.
- Communicating effectively is an essential function for a supervisor, manager or group leader.
- Report writing is an essential function of an analyst.

9.2 Workers with disabilities find more acceptance in the work force

A major transportation company headquartered in Los Angeles reports a positive experience with employing people with disabilities. Its human resources representatives say they need everybody's talent to be successful in the coming years, and they cannot afford to discount any group just because they're different. This company has been hiring workers with disabilities for many years, and they have employed many excellent workers with disabilities, like Bob.

By the time he was 28, Bob had established himself as a high achiever who excelled in sports and was particularly fond of swimming and surfing. Ironically, it was a diving accident that ended his career as a policeman and left him a wheelchair user with impaired mobility. After learning to manage the equipment and specially fitted van that gave him mobility, his former job enabled him to enter a special program to be retrained as a computer programmer. After he completed the training, the program's administrators helped him secure his first job with the transportation company, and within a few years his good performance led to a promotion as a senior systems analyst.

The transportation company's Equal Opportunities Affairs manager reports that Bob's case is only unusual in that they were aware of his disability because it was visible. The company usually does not find out a person has a disability unless the individual requests some special accommodation.

This company's experience with accommodation has been slight and is consistent with national studies. Those studies show that only 10 percent of accommodations made for people with disabilities cost more than $1,000; 60 percent cost less than $1,000; and 30 percent cost nothing.

The most common types of accommodations for persons with disabilities include making facilities accessible, restructuring a job so that it can be approached differently, modifying work schedules and acquiring or modifying equipment. For example, employees may require a certain kind of headset to use the telephone, an instrument to reach the computer keys, a computer screen that offers large type or a raised desk.

For companies that have already demonstrated success in integrating people with disabilities into the work force, the American Disabilities Act represents not so much a change in policy as much as a change in procedures. They have gotten past the erroneous and incorrect misconception that people with disabilities have high absence rates and are difficult to manage. They recognize that people with disabilities want to be productive members of society.

9.3   Handling the interview and employment process

If you have declared a disability to a prospective employer (a lot of people do not), you should be knowledgeable about your rights and know what to expect in the interview and employment process. It is important that under all circumstances you approach the employer with a positive attitude and project a professional image befitting the position.

Regarding the interview

1. The interviewer may ask questions about your ability to perform the essential duties of the job but should not ask about your disability. For instance: "How will you operate this equipment?" not "Would your disability interfere with your operating this equipment?" You should be prepared to answer this question, even if the interviewer asks it incorrectly. A "Yes, I can operate the equipment" is insufficient. You should be prepared to explain how and give examples of when you have operated that kind of equipment.

2. The interviewer may ask questions about your ability to develop effective interpersonal relationships on the job. You should be prepared with examples of how you have worked effectively with others to accomplish tasks and projects. If the interviewer does not mention this aspect of the job, ask about teamwork so you get a chance to give examples of your interpersonal effectiveness.

3. The interviewer may ask questions about your initiative and motivational level. For instance: "If you were in a

situation where _____, how would you handle it?" Be prepared to draw on examples from past jobs and incidents dealing with effectively handling your disability to demonstrate your initiative, motivation and administrative skills.

4. The interviewer may ask questions about your energy level. For instance: "Sometimes the projects get pretty demanding. How would you handle a tight deadline or a temporarily heavy workload to meet an emergency need?" You should discuss some situations you've handled that required a lot of energy or involved multiple challenges. Again, it would be acceptable to draw from situations related to your disability if they are appropriate.

Questions the interviewer can and cannot ask

An employer can ask...

"Can you perform the duties of the position, with or without reasonable accommodation?" (However, a qualified applicant's inability to perform a nonessential function may not be considered in making a hiring decision.)

but not...

"Are you handicapped?" or *"Do you have a disability?"*

An employer can ask...

"Describe or demonstrate how you can operate a computer using only one hand" or (to a person with one leg) *"Demonstrate or explain how you will transport yourself and your tools downstairs, with or without reasonable accommodation."*

but not...

"How severe is your disability?", *"How did you become disabled?"* or *"How long have you been disabled?"*

Regarding your rights

1. The interviewer must explain the essential functions of the job and then ask if you can perform each of those functions. If the interviewer does not bring this up, you should ask what the essential functions are. You may not be disqualified because of your ability to perform any other function except the essential functions of the job.

2. If you need a special accommodation, you should request it. The interviewer should focus only on the request and not the disability or the medical reasons for the disability.

3. The interviewer may not disqualify you for an inability to perform an essential function of the job without the company first considering a reasonable accommodation.

4. You are not required to undergo a medical examination because of a disability before a job offer is made. However, a job offer may be contingent upon a medical evaluation, as well as education and reference checks. You can only be required to take a medical exam if everyone who receives a job offer is subject to that requirement.

5. An alcohol test is considered a medical exam. As a result, employers may no longer require applicants to undergo a combination drug and alcohol screen before a job offer is made. An alcohol screen may be given only after an offer is made to an applicant. (A drug screen is not considered a medical exam and still may be given at any point during the preemployment process.)

9.4   Organizations for assistance

If you need additional information, contact one of the following organizations:

Equal Employment Opportunity Commission Hotline
800-669-3362

National Information Center for Independent Living
602-256-2245

Job Accommodation Network
800-526-7234
or 800-ADA-WORK

National Institute of Disability and Rehabilitation Research
202-732-1184

Special Needs Information Referral Center
800-426-2133

Resolutions

1. The Americans With Disabilities Act (ADA) protects those with visible and nonvisible disabilities by ensuring an equal employment opportunity.

2. Under ADA, individuals with disabilities have the right to "reasonable accommodation," any reasonable change that would allow the individual to perform a job.

3. A disabled job seeker is not obliged to reveal the disability in a job interview, resume or job application.

4. The ADA requires that employees with disabilities receive equitable pay for comparable work.

5. A disability need not be an impediment to handling a lot of jobs, as long as the disability does not interfere with the essential tasks associated with the job.

6. Do not assume that a prospective employer would automatically be resistant to hiring a person with a disability. Studies have shown that the attendance records of individuals with disabilities are better than average and that their turnover rate is lower than average.

7. While the ADA has helped unplug some of the avenues to employment, each individual is responsible for his or her own success on the job.

8. Be prepared to explain in an interview how you will go about doing the job, how you get along with others and your level of motivation.

9. One of the most important factors for being successful is fitting in with the other employees. Since others are usually afraid of saying or doing the wrong thing, it's helpful if the person with the disability is the first to extend themselves in friendship.

Chapter 10

I don't have a degree

A college or postgraduate degree is a requirement for many jobs (try getting a position as a neurosurgeon with a high school diploma). In addition, there are other fields where a degree, while not being an absolute prerequisite, seems to provide easier access to good jobs. For example, while you may be a natural born salesperson, the individual with the business degree may have an edge on you in landing that account executive position.

Indeed, it's probably an understatement to say that a college degree doesn't hurt your chances of landing a job. And your lack of higher education may often hold you back. There are a few solutions to this problem. The first is to get a degree.

10.1 On the job and back to school

"That's the third time I've been passed over for a promotion," Joan wailed to her friend Barbara. "What's the sense of trying? It looks like I'll never get a promotion at this company."

Joan and Barbara both accepted jobs at about the same time in the human resources department of a large manufacturing company. They both had been hard workers, but Barbara had received two promotions during the five years they'd been with the company, while Joan's career seemed to be at a standstill.

"I'm probably not advancing because I don't have a degree. You know how this company is about that." She said, looking slightly annoyed. "It's dumb, really. You don't need a degree to advance in this department."

"Are you sure that having a degree is the issue? Look at me—I don't have one."

"Yes, but you're working on one, and they know it."

"Well, if you think it's important, why don't you work on one, too?"

"Barbara, that would take forever—going to school at night. I just don't know if I have the time, and besides, I'd be 37 by the time I finished."

"Look, Joan, if you believe you need to have a degree to succeed in this company, then you either have to get one or look for a place to work where it's not necessary. And most companies today want their professional employees to have a degree, so there's no point in changing companies."

For many companies the criteria for promotion includes a degree, regardless of whether you can show the equivalent knowledge through your experience. Therefore, it is prudent to research a company's policy before accepting a job, so you will understand what avenues for advancement will be opened or closed to you.

Obtaining a degree while holding down a full-time job is difficult and requires a tremendous commitment in time, especially if you have other priorities that have to be juggled. But if you start making the effort and show that you are willing to persevere, it may pay off for you in promotional opportunities even *before* you receive that diploma.

If you are in the midst of earning a degree while working, it's to your advantage to keep your supervisor posted as to your educational advancement. Let him or her know about the new skills you are acquiring, and you may be given the opportunity to exercise them in on-the-job projects. Your enthusiasm and motivation will be appreciated and possibly rewarded.

As even those who've earned college or postgraduate degrees are discovering, any career requires a commitment to continually learn to stay abreast of the field. If you are not motivated to make the sacrifices to develop your current career, it may be because you are not doing something you truly enjoy. You may want to rethink your career direction. (See Section 1.4.)

10.2 Check into your company's tuition reimbursement program

After working as a legal secretary for almost 10 years, Karen decided she wanted to become an attorney. She knew it would be a long haul, going to school at night, to say nothing of the expense. But she had a plan.

She quit her job with a small law firm and accepted a position in the corporate legal division of a large company. The company's 80-percent tuition reimbursement plan made a big dent in her tuition for law school.

Her employers, of course, were happy that she was working toward a law degree because it gave them a more valuable employee. They had more than a secretary; they had someone who could do research and handle a lot of the responsibilities of a paralegal.

In addition to getting most of her education paid for, Karen picked up valuable experience doing research—and she got two promotions during the time she worked for the company. She had to work pretty hard, but it was a win-win situation for everyone.

A few months before she was due to graduate from law school, the company had a layoff. She jumped at the chance to leave and receive severance pay. She was ready to start preparing to take the bar, and the time off with severance pay would provide her with a perfect time to study.

Her plan had worked out better than she dreamed.

It's not uncommon for large companies to offer some sort of tuition reimbursement program. Despite the expense, companies recognize that it's to their benefit to add to the skills and increase the value of their employees by furthering their education. As Karen's employers discovered, her law education allowed her to take on more research projects than she'd have been capable of before.

Check to see whether your current company (or if you're job hunting, the companies for which you're interviewing) offers a tuition reimbursement program and take advantage of it. Frequently, there are limitations. For example, the company will only pay for education that applies to its field, or it will only pay if you receive acceptable grades. But in most cases, such a program will provide you with a golden opportunity to increase your value to the company and to future employers.

10.3 Those who succeeded—without a degree

Apparently, college is not always a prerequisite for success. Look at the following list of some well-known people—without degrees—who have maximized the talents and gifts they were born with and persevered to achieve fabulous rewards.

Bill Gates
Cofounder, Microsoft Corporation
Dropped out of Harvard
Number one on Forbes 400
Estimated net worth: $6.3 billion

Ted Turner

Founder, Turner Broadcasting Systems
Owner, Atlanta Braves
Left Brown University during senior year
Estimated net worth: $1.9 billion

Russell Solomon

Founder, Tower Records
First sold records out of father's drugstore
Dropped out of high school
Yearly sales: $650 million

S. Daniel Abraham

Founder of Slim-Fast Foods and creator of Dexatrim
Skipped college for stint in army
Company earnings: more than $600 million

Jenny Craig

Cofounder, Jenny Craig, Inc., Weight Loss Centers
Did not complete college
Company sales: $461 million

Susie Tompkins

Cofounder, Esprit de Corps.
Introduced own name label
Dropped out of San Francisco Art Institute
Esprit sales: about $450 million

Frank Perdue

Founder, Perdue Chickens
Completed two-year teacher's college program
Estimated net worth: $300 million

Donna Karan

Clothing designer
Dropped out of Parson's School of Design
1992 company earnings: $270 million

Lillian Vernon

Founder, Lillian Vernon Corporation
Distributes 140 million catalogs annually
Dropped out of NYU
Company sales: $172 million

Penny Marshall
Actress, director
Dropped out of University of New Mexico
First female director to surpass $100 million for a film (Big)

Michael Moore
Documentary filmmaker/director
Dropped out of college
His 1989 film, Roger & Me, *cost $250,000 to make and grossed more than $8 million*

Larry King
Talk-show host, syndicated columnist, author of five books
Began working after high school
Estimated annual income: $2.5 million

Peter Jennings
Anchor and senior editor of *ABC's World News Tonight* since 1983
Dropped out of school after ninth grade
Awarded six Emmys for reporting

Maya Angelou
Poet
Never attended college
Wrote and recited "On the Pulse of Morning" for Clinton's inauguration

Barbara Bush
Dropped out of Smith College after sophomore year to marry George Bush
Former First Lady and author, Millie's Book

Jolene Unsoeld
Third-term Congresswoman from Washington State
Dropped out of Oregon State University
First woman to climb the north face of Grand Teton Mountain

10.4 Market yourself without a degree

If you feel that a formal course of study is not for you (and it's not for everyone), then it's still possible for you to achieve most career goals if you have enough drive and motivation to work hard. Be prepared for the fact that it may take you a little longer to get there, you may have to work harder at promoting yourself, but it can be done. The following steps will be helpful.

- Find out what kind of experience is necessary to succeed in the career you've chosen. Network with professionals who are doing what you want to do. Ask them to suggest jobs that will give you the experience you need. Also, be willing to do some independent reading and studying. The bookstores and libraries are full of self-help manuals and resource materials that can help supplement your on-the-job training.

- Be willing to gain experience in return for unpaid work. For example, if you're a typesetter who's interested in becoming a graphics designer, you might be able to get some hands-on experience laying out promotional brochures in return for doing the typesetting for the brochure copy. Look for apprenticeships and internships to gather experience.

- Use the skills you've developed to help get into the arena of your chosen profession. Get into the company you want to work for by using your existing marketable skills, then start networking to get into the career area you've chosen. (See Chapter 15.) For instance, you're an accountant and want to be a designer—work on getting an accounting job in a design house.

- When you get in the right company, request and be willing to volunteer for added responsibilities that will give you experience and provide accomplishments that will support your goal and that you can show on your resume.

- Structure your own training program designed to overcome your professional weaknesses and make you more marketable to employers. Take continuing education classes, and attend workshops and seminars by leaders in the fields in which you're interested. Seek advice from a professional in your field on workshops.

- Join associations that support your profession and participate in the training and network opportunities they afford.

- Look into a certification program that will give you added credibility but will not require as long of an educational commitment as pursuing a degree. Check with your local college, university or professional association about this type of program.

• After you've gained some experience (both on the job and in extracurricular activities) prepare a functional resume that will focus on accomplishments rather than job titles. (See Section 7.2.)

The reality of the situation is that in order to advance, even with a "natural gift," your talent will need the refinement, development and support that comes as a result of some type of education and training. Whether you opt for obtaining that education as part of a formal degree program or through specialized training, it must be done if you want your career to progress. Even those people who had a vision that led them to the top have had to pursue some additional training. In short, a college degree doesn't ensure you will get a job nor is it an absolute prerequisite for success, but the lack of higher education may often hold you back or make the process longer.

Resolutions

1. If you have determined that the only way to achieve your career goals is through a degree, then get it! Yes, it's quite a commitment, and it won't be easy to work and go to school at the same time. But in the long run, it will pay off.

2. Check into your company's tuition reimbursement program and see whether your company will pay to send you to school.

3. If you're currently interviewing for jobs, be sure to find out whether your prospective company offers tuition reimbursement.

4. Recognize that, in most cases, a college degree is not a prerequisite for career success. While it may not be easy, you may be able to achieve your career dreams without earning a degree.

5. Network with other professionals in your chosen field to determine what types of alternative experience might help you.

6. Read up on your chosen career, teach yourself as much as you can through resources at the library and through professional organizations.

7. Get involved in your field's professional organizations.

8. Look for apprenticeships, internships, volunteer experiences and other ways to gather unpaid experiences.

9. Be willing to "barter" for work experiences. For example, learn computer graphics in exchange for some accounting consultation.

10. Try to get into a company that offers jobs in your chosen field—even if your avenue into the company is in another area.

Chapter 11

I haven't worked in years

Typically, individuals who find themselves in this dilemma are women. They include stay-at-home moms whose last child has entered the first grade as well as older women who quit their last job to get married. And for a host of reasons—financial strain, death of a husband, divorce or personal fulfillment—they find themselves back in the job market.

Yet, today, another group of individuals is finding themselves in this situation. Women *and* men who may have retired a number of years ago are now finding that a job is necessary, either because they need the additional income or the mental stimulation.

Whatever your reasons for diving back into the job market, you may discover that you're ill-prepared. Having been out of the work force for so long, you may be rusty on the skills required to impress prospective employers. The most important of those skills will be addressed in this chapter.

11.1 Translate nonpaid experience into marketable skills

Linda called her friend Jane, a successful psychologist who'd been working in her career since the two had met in college.

"I need some advice. I'm 45, my daughter will be going to college in a year and John and I are divorced. Here I am with no work experience and no job skills. So now what do I do with the rest of my life?"

"What have you been doing up to this point?"

"Going to lunch with friends and playing bridge."

"Linda, you know that's not true. Every time I call you, you're busy with some committee or putting together a big fundraiser."

"Yes, but that's not *real* work. Now, I need to go back to work, but I am so out of touch with everything, I don't know if I can."

"Come on, Linda. You know how difficult it is to get a bunch of volunteers to do what you want them to do. You can certainly apply your organizational and motivational skills to the working world, too. You just have to know how to sell yourself."

Jane was right: Linda had gathered some impressive skills during the 20-year period she spent raising her family. While she didn't earn a penny for her efforts, Jane had taken on leadership roles in different volunteer organizations and community groups. She'd managed groups of volunteers, organized large events, been responsible for large amounts of money. She'd even learned how to use computers to create newsletters. With Jane's help, Linda reworked her resume, translating her volunteer experience into marketable skills that any employer would value.

Even if you haven't "worked" for years, you've undoubtedly gathered marketable skills that will enhance your value to prospective employers. It's an important exercise for you to assess these skills. Decide what you can do by looking at the things you've already done (see Chapter 1). Get input from friends and associates who may point out options and skills that you are taking for granted.

11.2 Build self-confidence through practice and preparation

Even with her resume completed, Linda was still hesitant to approach the job market.

"Jane, I still don't know if I have the confidence to approach an employer. What if I have to take a test or they ask me a question I can't answer? I don't even know how to interview. And what should I wear?" She rushed on in a panic. "This is all so overwhelming, I don't know if I can do it."

"Calm down, Linda. This is just like any other administrative project you've handled. You're going to do just fine. Okay, here's the action plan. Go down to the mall and get a couple of suits from that store that caters to career women. Let them guide you in the selection. Then go to the department store there and get a makeover."

"Why would I need suits? All I'll be applying for are assistant or clerical positions. I'm not looking to be a manager. Won't a nice dress do just as well?"

"Suits are the uniform of professionals and office workers. And you want to convey that you are serious. Then, with all your administrative experience, why don't you list with some temporary agencies and do some clerical work while you're making up your mind? That would be a great way to get in the business arena and start networking. And don't forget your contacts. You've worked with some of the biggest social service agencies in town. You already know enough people to network with to get work right now."

"I'm beginning to feel more encouraged. But I still need to know how to interview."

"Ask the personnel directors at a couple of the social service agencies to give you a practice interview. If they're not available, we could come up with a couple of other sources. Plus, the agencies will interview. So when you go for a permanent job, you'll be ready."

Linda took Jane's advice and found that one of the easiest ways for her to access opportunities was working as a temporary administrative assistant. On her last assignment, the employer liked her work so much that he offered her a permanent job.

Develop several options for your skills by talking with professionals in your field of interest. This is also a very convenient way to let people know that you are available. Also, network with the contacts you made while involved in community activities. These can be some of the most valuable sources for accessing a position.

Above all, be committed to maximizing your talents. Get additional training if necessary. There are plenty of courses available for almost any subject. Set a career goal that reflects your skills, interests and lifestyle—and personal goals.

11.3 A resume that positions you as a professional

Just because you haven't had a paid job experience in years doesn't mean you can't put together a powerful resume. Especially if you've been active in volunteer or community organizations. If you've been particularly active, you can even consider using a chronological resume format, and list your volunteer activities, offices and achievements just as you would work experience. The thing to remember is to position your experience in a professional manner. For example, if you took care of children for working parents, refer to yourself as a "childcare provider" rather than a "baby sitter."

Be sure to include accomplishments achieved while working on projects not connected with a paid position. For instance:

• Recruited volunteers and formed a fundraising committee which raised the monies to pay for 300 football uniforms.

Often, a functional resume is helpful in presenting yourself if you've worked off and on. It allows you to show years of experience in the summary statement, or number of years a position was held following the position title. (See Section 6.2.)

Do use references from the group of people you've worked with to accomplish extracurricular projects or tasks. They can attest to your skills and working traits. The higher their position, the more credible they are likely to be to the prospective employer.

11.4 Do's and don'ts for the interview

- **Make sure your image is updated and professional.** Now is the time to get those new clothes. If unsure of the appropriate attire, take a working friend along when you shop or rely on the advice of the salesperson in a store that caters to professional people.

- **Do schedule "practice" interviews.** This is a must. It's almost certain that the style of interviewing has changed since you last looked for a job. One source for interview experience is with employment agency representatives. Another source is your professional friends who will probably be happy to role-play with you.

- **Show commitment to a career.** Employers, in addition to looking for committed workers, want to hire individuals who have confidence in themselves and their decisions. Not only do you want to show that you're committed to your prospective employer, you want to indicate that your decision *not* to work was a positive choice, too. Be prepared to show that your decision to step out of the job market was a positive and proactive choice. Responses along the lines of the examples below might be appropriate:

    "I decided to devote time to raising my family, and now I am in a position to devote quality time to my career."

    "I've always had a desire to sail the Caribbean, so I decided to take a few years to explore that dream. It was an unforgettable experience, and I even had a few travel articles published. Now I'm ready to focus on my career."

    "I made a decision to leave the work force to take care of my mother while she battled cancer. She was always there for me, and I wanted to be there for her. That time with her was priceless to me, and now I'm ready to resume my career."

- **Don't make your job appear subordinate to your spouse's career (even if it is).** A comment like, "My spouse was relocated so I was forced to give up my job," may cause your prospective boss to worry about your commitment, if your spouse were to be transferred again. Instead, respond by focusing on the enthusiasm you have for your new home—"We've always been attracted to the Southwest, so we sought out opportunities to make it happen."

- **Do have a career goal in mind.** Make sure you don't convey the impression that the position you're interviewing for is just a stop-gap measure for you. It's best if your career goal dovetails with the company with whom you are interviewing.

- **Do know something about the company.** Before the interview, visit the library and read up a little about the company or check with people in your network. At the very least, peruse the company information available in the reception area. Be able to at least ask a couple of questions about the company's products or services.

- **Do avoid references to personal situations.** Do not include information about your spouse, children or grandchildren in your introduction of yourself. For example, when the interviewer asks, "Tell me about yourself," say:

  "I've gained experience in business and the nonprofit sector. I've had an opportunity to organize and manage projects and budgets. I've been complimented on my interpersonal skills and my ability to handle multiple tasks at the same time. I'm looking forward to applying these skills again in the business arena."

Don't say:

"I worked for a short while a long time ago. Then I started doing volunteer work while raising my two children and taking care of my husband."

If the interviewer should bring up children, your husband or any personal situation during the interview, you may choose to give a short reply. But always bring the subject back to the interview. A good way of doing this is by asking a question about the job or company. Additionally, don't bring up transportation problems, the fact that your spouse may not like you to work overtime, your concerns about making ends meet since your spouse left you or since you retired. Keep it professional.

- **Know the appropriate range for your skills.** Prior to the interview, research salaries. You may be so happy just to have a salary, you could end up accepting less than you deserve. Some sources for salary information include: working friends who could check their companies' salary scale with the personnel office; positions advertised in the newspapers; temporary agencies; and library reference sources like *American Almanac of Salaries* and the *Occupational Compensation Survey*.

- **Do let the interviewer know you want the job.** A positive statement at the end of the interview will let you know where you stand. For example:

  You: "This sounds like a great job, and I think I'd like to work here. When will you be making your decision?"

  Interviewer: "Probably in about a week."

  You: "Would it be all right if I check back with you at that time?"

  Follow up the interview with a thank-you letter, and mention that you will call in a week or whatever was discussed.

The process of returning to a "paid" position is similar to riding a bicycle. Even if you haven't done it for a while, the skill will return as soon as you start the process. The differences between then and now may require adjustments in your resume style (companies expect to see accomplishments now), your dress and your expectations. But even these issues can be brought in line with the help of friends or career planning centers.

Resolutions

1. Enlist the help of friends and working professionals in analyzing your work and volunteer activities to determine your skills and set a goal.

2. Develop a functional resume that will allow you to show examples of skills gained through paid and nonpaid experiences.

3. Update your personal image so it reflects the type of job you want.

4. Do practice interviews with friends and professional associates.

5. Use paid and nonpaid sources as networking contacts.

6. Consider temporary agencies as an avenue to make money, gain experience and network into a permanent job.

7. Be willing to get additional training if needed. Everyone needs some computer skills. These skills may be obtained through a high school adult education class or through a community college. The fees are usually nominal.

8. Know a salary range you can quote for your skills, and ask for the job.

Chapter 12

I can't find a job in my field

You've scoured the want ads, checked industry publications, called corporations and sent out an avalanche of resumes—and you still can't seem to drum up any good job leads. Now what do you do?

12.1 Step in and fill an existing need

Donna had been looking for a job for more than four months after being laid off from her middle management position in a large manufacturing company. She had networked with all her friends and former co-workers, responded religiously to every ad she saw and followed up leads. It seemed that there were plenty of jobs available—just none in her field.

She decided to try a search firm. The waiting room at the agency was chaotic. The receptionist had just quit. Phones were ringing and counselors were trying to interview clients, while people were milling around looking frustrated because they weren't being helped.

Finally, after observing the confusion, Donna's natural take-charge instincts took over. She stepped behind the receptionist desk and started fielding calls. Within an hour she had a handle on the situation. She knew the counselors' schedules and had a list of the people in the waiting room, including their needs and occupations. As the counselors finished with each candidate, they were able to pick up the next person by looking at the list she had prepared. Once the candidates realized they were going to be helped, they calmed down and order was restored to the reception area.

As for Donna, by the end of the day she had been offered and accepted a job as receptionist. While the position was not what she had been looking for, the opportunity put her in a position where she could learn about the companies that were hiring people in her field. She was happy to gather information as a temporary fill-in for the agency.

If you observe a situation in which you can step in and fill a need, seize the opportunity. At the very least, it will put you in a position to meet new people with whom you can network.

12.2 Expand your network

For 12 years, Adrian held a well-paying job monitoring system computer operations in a technical company that handled highly classified information. Her social contacts were few, since she worked by herself on the midnight to 8 a.m. shift and slept most of the daylight hours. When she was forced to seek another position, she didn't know how to start networking.

Her opportunity to meet more people came through her niece who suggested that she start selling beauty products. She told the one or two customers she had that she would give them a special gift if they hosted a beauty party for her and invited at least 10 people. While socializing at the parties, she grasped every opportunity to let everyone know that she was looking for a full-time job and what her skills were. After three parties, she knew quite a few more people, and eventually one of her customers told her about an opening in her husband's company.

Are there really no jobs to be found in your field? Not likely. You're probably just not hearing about them. So you need to take steps to widen your networking net. First, broaden your network. Make contacts with other professionals in your field through past work relationships (talk to vendors and clients as well as associates). Also talk with friends and relatives. Word-of-mouth is how most positions are filled, before the job opening is ever advertised. That's why it's important that you have as many contacts as possible to hear about the jobs in your field, before others do.

12.3 Broaden your thinking

When Kari, a producer of documentaries, had exhausted all of his networking contacts, he decided to attend his professional association's quarterly meeting. Maybe he would meet someone there who could give him a lead to an opportunity for producing documentaries.

Susan turned out to be the contact. "Kari, what have you been doing for the past year since we last talked?"

"For six months of that time I've been looking for a job."

"It's great that we ran into each other, then. I know a company that is looking for someone to assist in their in-house production department working on corporate films and sales materials."

"You're kidding. Get dressed up in a gray suit every day and work in a stuffy corporate environment? I couldn't bear it. Besides, I make documentaries, not corporate films."

"I think you could stand it. You'd only have to wear a suit to the interview, as anyone would. The other people in the production department dress as you do now, and no doubt you would fit comfortably into the culture."

"You're right. I think I'll give it a try. Who knows, I might like it."

Perhaps you're not recognizing opportunities because your definition of your "field" is too narrow. Kari was only pursuing independent film production companies—of which there were few in his area. Susan encouraged him to broaden his search by exploring corporations that might have their own production departments.

12.4 Don't label yourself too narrowly

Marcie had more than 15 years of experience in the insurance industry. Most of that time had been spent processing claims, except for the beginning of her career, which included some light accounting and bookkeeping. Now she was ready to move on, but she didn't know where to go.

With the insurance industry seeming to be in a depressed hiring state, Marcie told her contacts she didn't know what to do.

"First of all," Morris said, "stop describing yourself as 'a person with 20 years of insurance experience, and that's all I know.' It's too narrow and does not give people enough information to help you."

"But it's true," she insisted. "All I know is insurance."

"It would be better if you said you had 20 years' administrative experience in a heavy processing environment. That you can handle difficult customers, solve workload and people problems and are good with details. That would give you more options for finding a job, because those are skills that could be transferred to a lot of jobs."

"Like what jobs?"

"How about a newspaper, publishing company, hospital, doctor's office, retail or banking industries?"

"Those are good ideas. Thanks."

Your job goal may be so narrowly defined that you only respond to job openings with specific titles. Instead, think about the skills you use in your job, and see if those don't transfer to some other job titles. This effort may require some self-assessment, and research of other fields and job descriptions as well.

12.5 Get your foot in the door

"What are you doing here, Nancy?" Amy asked when she saw her friend working at the information desk in the telephone company.

"I'm working here now. Have been for about three months now."

"But weren't you in charge of telecommunication services at your last company?"

"Yes, I was. And I still would like to get back into that function, but I haven't been able to find anything yet. So in the meantime, the temp agency sent me here. At least I'm in a telecommunications environment."

"What about the pay? It must be a lot less."

"It is. But I know how to manage with less. The good part about this job is that it's in the right environment, and I might be able to eventually move into what I want to do. The pay will come. You know I'm a practical person."

If you want a position in a particular area and are not finding jobs in that area, consider checking out companies that have similar or related products or services. You will likely find one that is growing and hiring people in other areas. If you're fortunate enough to find one that likes to promote from within and encourages employee growth, you could take a job in one area, with plans to move into your chosen field. Being inside the company, you're positioned to be one of the first people who hears about openings when they do come up.

12.6 Create your own opportunities

Meryl's desire was to be a writer for a major corporation, but her journalism degree was not sufficient without some practical experience, especially when responding to ads. So she set out to get the experience.

She wrote a book review geared for the audience of her local paper, and it was accepted. She was not only paid but offered a job of writing reviews. She was working as an independent contractor, but that was fine. She was getting experience. She signed up with a temporary agency that supplied administrative help to the major corporations in her area. She used each temporary assignment as an opportunity to network. And she got a few writing projects that way. But her biggest break came when *The Wall Street Journal* published one of her articles. She believes this was the accomplishment that helped get her a job as an assistant writer with a mid-sized company.

If you truly have your heart set on a particular field, but you just can't find an opening, create your own work. Volunteer. Become an independent contractor. Seek out needs and fill them.

The simple key to eliminating the roadblocks to finding a job in your field may be just to modify or expand your approach. When you're stuck, it may be time to stop spinning your wheels, reassess and be willing to move in some other directions in order to accomplish your career goal.

Resolutions

1. Networking is one of the best ways of finding out about jobs in your field. Review the sources you have contacted, and contact people you overlooked or thought would not be good contacts.

2. Look for opportunities to add new contacts to your network. Take a class or involve yourself in a new activity you've always wanted to try as an avenue for meeting new people.

3. Don't put yourself in a box by limiting the definition of your capabilities to an industry or job title; expand your opportunities by describing your capabilities through transferable skills.

4. When opportunities are presented, be willing to explore them—especially for the possibility of using them as a stepping stone to what you want to do.

5. First, *get in* a company, accepting whatever reasonable position you can fill. Then seize every opportunity to work your way into the job you *really* want.

6. Be proactive by creating your own opportunities. Seek out needs and fill them.

Chapter 13

I'm a technical person

As a technical person, particularly one with a lot of experience, you have some special challenges to deal with in the job search process. The first one is getting your resume to the person who can make a hiring decision about you. Then, how much technical information should you include and how long should the resume be? You've probably heard that a resume should only be one page and are wondering how you can possibly get all your relevant experience on one page.

Then there are the stories you have heard about the interviewing process: that some interviews are being conducted by less experienced, or even nontechnical, staff; that some companies will try to get you without paying an appropriate salary for all your experience; and in some cases you'll be vastly overqualified for the positions that are available.

So how is a technical person, especially one with extensive experience, supposed to approach the market with some degree of success?

You can no longer rely solely on your skills and experience to ensure job consideration by the hiring manager. You'll most likely need to modify your resume and show adaptability in the interviewing process in order to have a positive impact on all the people who will influence the hiring decision.

13.1 How John got his resume past personnel

As soon as John, an information systems consultant, heard that the company planned to restructure its corporate headquarters and lay off a large percentage of the staff, he started preparing himself to find another position and sought out the assistance of his friend Joyce, a personnel rep for a human resources department.

Joyce laughed when she saw his resume. "John, you've got too much information and it's too long."

"But I won't get considered if I don't show all the necessary experience."

"You won't get considered at all if you can't get your resume past personnel. Trust me, after they've gone through hundreds of resumes a day, they won't want to try to decipher this epic. They may not know the meaning of a lot of these terms you use or how your experience would fit with their requirements."

"All I thought they did was pass it on to the manager."

"John," she said, surprised, "sometimes I receive hundreds of resumes when we post an opening. The manager is not about to read all those resumes. He expects me to screen them and forward the best candidates to him."

"You mean my resume has got to appeal to you *and* to the manager?"

"It does if you want to get it past personnel. First of all, it's important to translate technical terms into generic language for the nontechnical person like me, and to make the terms in the body of the resume match the terms in the ad, so I know there's a match when I'm screening. You may know that a particular term means the same as another—but I might not, and because of that your resume might not get referred."

Joyce then helped John rewrite his resume into one that would be workable for responding to ads. Joyce convinced John to use a functional format to avoid the repetition in the four-page resume, and thereby reduced his resume to two pages. The new resume follows on the next two pages.

13.2 Chronological versus functional resume

While it is necessary to prepare a resume that will get past personnel, you want your resume to also be acceptable to the hiring manager. If your research and networking indicates that the hiring manager would expect a chronological resume rather than a functional one, then you should plan to use that preferred style.

Both resume styles should have a statement at the top that summarizes overall years of experience, key knowledge areas and strengths. If your profession encompasses a lot of technical terms that are referred to often, such as computer software or hardware terms, it is acceptable to summarize that information on an addendum sheet. Thus, you may end up with a two-page resume, plus a sheet of terms, and that is acceptable.

John's "nontech-friendly" resume

John Scott
1000 Houston Avenue
Glendale, CA
(300) 555-8773

Summary

A results-oriented professional with more than 15 years of experience in the management and administration of system development projects and staffs. Expertise is broad in scope, including PC/LAN, client/server and mainframe platforms. Excellent negotiation skills and track record for getting the job done right.

Accomplishments

Management and Administration

- Conducted study to identify PC/LAN-based Tax Return system.
- Coordinated implementation of Novell LAN's in Los Angeles, Denver, Kentucky and Atlanta.
- Directed, managed and participated in the development of tax return-related applications including bridges/interfaces between platforms and systems (e.g., mainframe PPE to FAMS).
- Planned and participated in the conversion of a major tax department to a Windows-based environment. This included hardware memory upgrades, installation of Windows and the Microsoft suite of programs (Word, Excel, Powerpoint, Mail).
- Played a key role in decision to implement a company's Wide Area Network.
- Researched, acquired and implemented a networked CD-ROM environment for tax research activities.
- Developed, tested and implemented many Clipper applications.
- Extensive knowledge of Novell's Systems Administration Functions.

Client/Server Environment

- Acquisition of HP/9000 G30 Data Base Server running HP/UX.
- Set up client environment using the Novell network and Novell's LAN Workplace for DOS (TCP/IP).
- Installed Microsoft Access version 2.0 and wrote small application accessing a Sybase Data Base.
- Coordinated preparation of project plan for rolling out client/server platform for a corporate division.

(continued)

John Scott
page 2

Additional Information

• Attended Fast Track to Sybase 10, and Sybase 10 Data and System Administration classes.

• Expertise in OS/JCL and COBOL.

• Extensive knowledge of both PC hardware and software, having worked with PCs since 1981.

• Experienced in developing applications in dBASE.

Professional History

1982—1994	PAGE Company, Los Angeles, Calif. **Manager,** New Technologies **Manager,** Tax Systems Group **Senior Consultant**
1980—1982	Independent Contractor, Los Angeles, Calif. **Systems Consultant**
1979—1980	BRUEWAY, Inc., Los Angeles, Calif. **Manager,** Systems and Development
1969—1979	Brown Bank, Los Angeles, Calif. **Manager,** Demand Deposit, Accounting Applications **Programmer/Analyst/Project Manager**
1967—1969	General Telephone Company, Los Angeles, Calif. **Programmer**

Education

1967   B.S. Mathematics, Northern Arizona University, Flagstaff, Ariz.

Whether responding to an ad or sending an unsolicited resume to a company, you should include a cover letter. The cover letter is another vehicle (along with the summary statement) for writing your qualifications so they'll be easily understood by nontechnical people. The language used in the cover letter should be generic and appeal to the nontechnical personnel person who needs to quickly assess your qualifications for referral to a manager. This is especially important when responding to an advertised position with a chronological resume that includes a lot of technical terms.

13.3 Dress to impress

One of the reasons Peter was attracted to the software company was because of its casual environment. He believed it would be a place where he could relax and really accomplish something as an engineer.

When the personnel manager contacted him for an interview, he was told it would be casual and to come in on a Saturday morning. When Peter arrived that morning in a leisure suit, he was surprised to see the manager dressed in a dark suit and tie. The manager's comment to Peter was, "I see you decided to dress casually." What the manager had meant by "casual" was that the interview would be on a Saturday instead of a regular workday. Peter completed the interview, but he was uncomfortable and felt awkward. He felt he had not projected the image he needed to.

A lot of technical environments are very casual, with management and workers dressing in a similar relaxed fashion. In some, you may never even have to wear a jacket. But, regardless of the norms of the business, you should always wear a suit and tie to an interview. It is the uniform of business, and there are no exceptions—whether on a regular workday, a Saturday or at an off-premise location like a restaurant.

It is a good idea to be prepared to be interviewed by technical as well as nontechnical people, possibly in tandem or in a group situation. You may not find this out until you arrive or until you pass the first interview stage and are asked to meet with other people in the company who will be offering input into the hiring decision. Therefore, you want to be dressed in a suit and be able to convey a polished, professional image to everyone.

13.4 Interviewing

"That's the third interview I've blown," said Paul, a senior engineer, to his friend Tom, a fellow engineer. They had both been looking for positions for three months and were having their weekly breakfast meeting to discuss their progress.

"What do you think is happening?"

"Actually, each case was different. I blew the first interview over salary. Apparently I wanted a whole lot more than they were willing to pay."

"Did you know going into the interview what they wanted to pay?"

"I had an idea, but I figured they would still have to pay me a certain amount. After all, I am a senior engineer with 20 years of experience. But I was wrong. I could sort of tell by how the interviewer reacted to my salary quote." Paul sighed deeply, "Anyway, I never heard from them again."

"What happened with the second interview?"

"The interviewer kept asking me questions about test, and I kept emphasizing design. I think they were looking for a test engineer."

"And the third interviewer?"

"I really blew that one out of the water. They put me in a conference room and brought this young kid in to interview me. He didn't know anything, and he kept asking me elementary questions. I was highly insulted, and I let him know that." He sheepishly looked down at the table. "I guess I could have handled that situation a little better."

"Well, at least we know your resume is working. I sure miss the days when you could walk into a stable company and get a decent job."

"Yep. So do I."

Just as you maintain and update your knowledge of the technical aspects of your profession, you'll have to update your knowledge of the employment process. Once, the demand for technical people was so high that securing premium positions with high pay was expected. But the shifting global priorities within the last decade, combined with outsourcing and the competition for available slots, has reduced opportunities and salaries.

It is now necessary to strategize more to accomplish your goals. Be guided by the interviewer's questions and responses to your inquiries. If a company seems to offer the potential for you to accomplish your goals, be willing to compromise on initial salary and responsibilities during the interview, especially if your research has shown that the salary fits the norm for the area. Also, improve your communication and negotiation skills through practice interviews—with peers as well as with older or younger interviewers. The team orientation of business today demands that you be able to demonstrate those good social skills before an offer is made.

Once inside the company, you can look for ways of working within the structure to achieve your goals.

Using these kinds of competitive techniques in your job change process and accepting the necessity of appealing to nontechnical, as well as technical people with less experience, will put you in the position to be considered for the jobs you seek.

Resolutions

1. While there is a general feeling among resume screeners that resumes should be no longer than two pages, it is not unusual for a technical person to have a two- to three-page resume. Even so, including a summary statement (stressing generic terms) at the top of a detailed resume will satisfy both the human resource professional for screening and the technical manager for detail, thus increasing your likelihood of being called for an interview.

2. A functional resume is usually quite effective for a person who has a lot of experience, but the norms of your technical field should be the final standard for choosing your resume format. There are some technical environments where the hiring manager would want to see the experience broken down chronologically. Even in those instances it is still necessary to include a summary statement to make the screening process easier for the personnel person.

3. Most technical environments have a casual work environment, but with the advent of the panel interview encompassing both technical and nontechnical members, it is important to dress in a polished, professional way to impress all interviewers with your appearance. Wear a nice suit.

4. If you are an experienced person, and your research (networking) prior to an interview reveals that the general age group of its workers is younger than yourself, expect that they may be less knowledgeable, and never, ever be condescending to the interviewer.

5. Expect employers to interview you for specific work and for the salary that fits those specific skills, not necessarily considering your past salary, which may have been for more skills and experience.

6. Not only are technical people expected to have the requisite skills, they're increasingly required to exhibit social skills, as well. More demand for interaction with other departments—as well as clients—means an increased demand for good communication skills.

7. Understand that companies are not hiring robots for technical positions. It may seem irrelevant to the job, but expect questions geared to determine your ability to fit into their culture, particularly from the nontechnical interviewers. Treat these questions seriously.

8. In some technical professions, basic tests will be administered. At the time the interview is scheduled, ask about the process and if tests will be given so you will be prepared.

Chapter 14

I've made mistakes in the past

Have you done something either on or off the job that would have a negative impact on your chances of being hired or promoted? Perhaps you've been fired—maybe even more than once—or you have a criminal record in your past or a long history of short-lived jobs that makes your resume look like a game of hopscotch. Whatever your past mistakes, you've overcome your problems and have a new positive outlook and goals for a productive work life.

That's the good news. The bad news is that your clouded history may prevent you from getting on the right track—as employers are reluctant to hire or promote you. There are ways to improve your chances, however.

14.1 If you were fired once...

Tony decided to take responsibility for his life, almost as a last resort, following a series of disastrous personal and professional events that ended in job termination.

As a teenage father, Tony dropped out of school to get married and support a family. As the demands of new parenthood and being the sole financial support of three people took its toll, Tony's work performance started to deteriorate. After staying up all night with a fussy baby, Tony often arrived at work two or three hours late. He'd frequently fall asleep on the job or make mistakes in his work. Eventually, his supervisor confronted him about his performance. But Tony, already panicked about all his new responsibilities, tried to cover up or deny his mistakes. Within six months, he was fired.

At first Tony blamed his supervisor, the company, his wife and the world in general for his dismissal. After some personal reflection aided by discussions with friends, he eventually accepted responsibility for his discharge and was able to get another job and start a new career direction.

Being fired can have a devastating impact on your self-esteem as well as your financial status. But it certainly doesn't mean you'll never find work again! Handled properly, you can overcome much of the negative affect of a termination.

If you have been fired, it's not necessary to say so on your resume. But expect to address the issue on your application form and in the interview. You must be honest. On your application, simply state "employment terminated," when asked to give reason for leaving.

In the interview, you will undoubtedly be asked why you were fired. Be prepared. Don't lay blame—even if it really *wasn't* your fault. Answers like, "The management was taking bribes, and I confronted them about it," "My boss was harassing me sexually," "My co-workers were incompetent and they resented me" raise red flags that cause interviewers to back off quickly.

It's best to avoid too much detail. You're not obligated to spill your guts and rehash every painful detail. But you must be honest. If you were fired for poor attendance, for instance, just indicate this, then give examples of how you've overcome this problem. You'll make the greatest impression on an interviewer if you show that you accept responsibility for the termination and point out achievements since them. Here are two examples of responses that might prove effective:

> *"I was inexperienced in the ways of the workplace. I didn't understand what was expected of me and, thus, failed to meet the expectations of my supervisor. Since that time, I've learned how important it is to clearly establish job descriptions and goals with my boss. In fact, in my last job, I achieved..."*

> *"I was going through a difficult time and missed quite a bit of work. I feel badly about letting my boss and co-workers down, and now I realize how important it is to assume responsibility for my workload. In the meantime, my temp jobs have given me the opportunity to exercise this responsibility. In fact, on my last job, my supervisor praised my efforts and said she wished her permanent staff had such commitment."*

14.2 If you've had a long history of job failures...

At 34, Eddie was still living the social life he began as a college student. He continued with weekend drinking binges, which often started midweek, and often smoked marijuana when he wanted to relax at the end of a stressful day.

Eddie's mechanical skill, plus an outgoing personality, always enabled him to get a job. The problem was his inability to *keep* the job because of poor performance and attendance. His cycle was predictable. Drug abuse led to poor attendance, which led to a negative review and finally to termination.

After being fired several times, Eddie acknowledged his problem. He sought treatment and after completing a recovery program, he returned to the job market to find work. It wasn't easy finding an employer who wanted to risk hiring him. But Eddie persevered, adding to his skills and experience through some volunteer activities with drug rehabilitation programs. He restructured his resume, leaving off several of the jobs that lasted only weeks or months. Eventually, he found an employer who recognized his sincerity and commitment to turning his life around, and Eddie developed into a productive and valued worker.

When you've had an erratic job history, marred by several terminations and negative reports, you face a real challenge in presenting yourself as a reliable and desirable employee. But it's not impossible. Here are some hints:

If you've had a series of jobs, it is best to eliminate dates of employment from your resume as much as possible and show total experience in a summary similar to the job-hopper's resume shown in Chapter 5.

If you've had many short-lived jobs of, say, less than a few months, it might make sense to eliminate some of these—especially if you left under negative circumstances. On the application, you'll have to show dates, and you should write "employment terminated" as your reason for leaving positions from which you were fired. Expect to address the issue of frequent job change in the interview. When questioned, you'll leave the best impression with the employer if you take responsibility for the poor job performance, show what achievements you've made since then and tell what steps (counseling or a program) you have taken to eliminate the cause of the recurring problem.

14.3 If you have a criminal record...

Sonya's wild teen years led her into a life of petty crime that resulted in incarceration for a felony during her early 20s. With the assistance of an agency and some friends, she was eventually able to land a decent job after her release.

After five years on the job, she decided to try for a better opportunity she heard about in another company. She felt her chances would be better if she did not mention the felony, so she left it off her application. She was hired. After 18 months and good performance reviews, she felt comfortable bidding on a promotional opportunity advertised in the company newsletter.

She was never given a chance for an interview. She was called to the personnel office and asked about the felony arrest and conviction earlier in her life. She confessed that she had lied on her application but hastened to point out that she had been a good citizen since then and had performed well on the job. The personnel manager commented that if she had truly been a good citizen, she would have told the truth on her application. Because of her work performance, the management opted to let her retain her position, but she was eliminated from consideration for the promotional opportunity.

It is not necessary to mention a criminal record on a resume, but *always* tell the truth about it when the information is requested on an application form or in an interview. The prospective employer has the right to verify any information that you put on the application. A falsehood can be grounds for immediate termination—no matter when it's uncovered.

If your record is brought up in an interview, accept responsibility for your actions, and then go on to speak about your achievements since then. The law prohibits the employer from questioning you about arrests, so it's not necessary for you to indicate what the crime was.

Unfortunately, determining whether to hire an applicant who answers "yes" is a very subjective task. In evaluating an applicant with a felony conviction, the employer generally considers the nature and number of convictions, when the convictions occurred, how the convictions relate to the job and whether the applicant appears to be rehabilitated. If you have questions about your rights contact The Equal Employment Opportunity Commission at 800-669-3362.

14.4 If a negative reputation prevents you from advancing in your company...

"I should have gotten that job," Tracy complained bitterly to her friend Jean about the clerical job she had missed out on.

"I was the most qualified. I have more years of service and all the experience they asked for. I think they're playing favorites."

"Come on, Tracy. Be fair. You don't know that they played favorites. Did you talk with the manager?"

"No. It's not going to make any difference what he says anyway."

"I think you owe it to yourself to find out the reasons the other candidate was chosen over you. You're not afraid to ask him, are you?" Jean said with a challenging look.

"Of course not. I'll ask him, if for no other reason than to shut you up."

After agreeing to meet with her, Ed gave Tracy an apprehensive look as she walked into his office for their appointment. She quickly put his fears to rest. "Mr. Danthrop, I'm not here to complain about not getting the position. I'm here to get some feedback from you about what I could do to be more competitive for the next position."

Ed relaxed. "I'll be glad to give you some feedback on why I chose the other candidate. I assume you want me to be very candid."

"Yes, I do."

"Tracy, you have a reputation in the company for having a bit of a negative attitude. There was a write-up in your personnel file from your supervisor about your attitude. Your records also show that you have had poor attendance and you're often late. Those things make us wonder how committed you are."

Tracy felt it would do no good to argue. Everything he said was true. "You're right. I have had a bad attitude. I've been bored on the job, and I know that I need a challenge. That was why I applied for your opening. I've always wanted to work in this area, and I know that I would do a good job."

"From the other reports I've received on your performance, I would tend to agree with that, Tracy. But if you want to get ahead, you've also got to establish a positive attitude and work ethic."

"You're right. I did some research on you before the interview, too. I heard that you're a fair person, so I'd like to propose this: I'll clean up my act and tow the line. When you have another opening, will you consider me then?"

He seemed pleased with her response. "I certainly will."

Later, Tracy told Jean, "I've decided to get my act together. I want a career and I'm willing to do what is necessary to have one."

Tracy worked at changing her attitude, and within nine months she had a clerical job in Ed's department.

People within a company can easily secure information about your performance, even if there is no information in your personnel file. It's easy to call your supervisors and others you've worked with to get a true picture of your performance and attitude. A negative reputation is not fatal. It can generally be changed, through time, with effort and good performance.

14.5 A problem resolution model

Step 1. Accept that you have a problem.

It is not uncommon to deny a troublesome situation or to insist that it's not as severe as it may seem. But when friends and family members are telling you a problem exists, when co-workers indicate subtly or directly that a situation is interfering with your performance (poor performance reviews are a strong indicator) or when a situation prevents you from accomplishing your goals, then you must accept that you have a problem.

Step 2. Develop options for addressing the problem.

Sometimes we deny problems because we cannot figure out what we would do about them if we acknowledged them or because the solution seems overwhelming—or perhaps we're comfortable where we are and afraid to make a change. That's where friends, relatives and peers can again be helpful. Helping someone leaves the giver feeling wonderful, so others will usually be happy to help you come up with ways of addressing the problem.

Step 3. Choose the option that will best help you attain your goal.

Out of the options that are suggested to you, select three for consideration. Evaluate the pros and cons of each option against your goal. You may have to get more help from friends on this one. It's a good idea to write out the information in a chart form so that you can clearly see the possibilities with each option. The option you finally choose should not only be the one that will best help you attain your goal, it should be the one you can truly commit to.

Step 4. Develop a plan for change or correction.

Make a plan for implementing the option. Establish objectives that will allow for making small steps toward the goal. If the change seems overwhelming, you will tend to resist it. Commit to accomplishing one step at a time, and set completion dates for each step to help you progress steadily toward the goal.

Step 5. Modify your plan as needed along the way.

Your course should not be set in concrete. When situations or circumstances occur that affect your plan, be flexible enough to re-group and evaluate what changes need to be made to keep you on track and working toward your goal. The important thing is to never give up.

Step 6. Give yourself rewards for your accomplishments.

Build a reward system into your plan at each critical step. The rewards need not be elaborate—dinner out, weekend away, purchase of a desired object. But it is important to have positive feedback and reinforcement to keep you going.

Step 7. Reinforce your success by helping someone else.

There is no better way to learn or to reinforce a newly acquired skill than to teach someone else. Helping someone else will provide extra joy and enhancement to your accomplishment.

Resolutions

1. If you have made a mistake, acknowledge it. There are other people who have been persecuted for any number of reasons, but that should not be your first conclusion when a job situation does not work out. Always look first at your actions and what you have done to contribute to your downfall. Drugs, absenteeism, an argumentative attitude, poor performance are all factors that are within a person's individual control. When you mess up—accept responsibility for it.

2. For internal positions, where supervisors have access to your personnel file, do not argue about a poor performance review. Acknowledge it, and say that you are back on track now, giving them some examples of your new behavior. End of discussion.

3. As a rule, do not include references with your application. Wait until they are requested. Before giving the reference, discuss with that person what they plan to say. It is important to choose references who will support your changed behavior. After the interview, let the reference know immediately, so they can be prepared to respond accordingly by supporting your changed behavior (if that issue came up in the interview) as well as your capability of handling the job.

4. It is not mandatory to use your former supervisor as a reference. Most companies have a rule that supervisors are not to give references so to not use yours would not be considered negative. But it's possible that someone

might speak with your former supervisor through a networking contact. If that happens, you want the supervisor's report to at least be supportive. Talk with former employers, again accepting responsibility for any poor performance reviews, and ask if you can come to an agreement about the reference they would give for you, especially if you were fired. To help convince prospective employers of your rehabilitation, have several reputable references who will support that you are a changed person.

5. Develop a plan for your next career move. (See Section 1.6.) At the same time, if fired, consider temporary employment through an agency as an option until you can secure a permanent position. A listing of permanent and temporary placement agencies is available under the employment section in the yellow pages of the telephone directory. Sign up with as many temporary agencies as you can and use those temporary assignments as one avenue for networking into a permanent job. Working through an agency will also serve as a good employer source when listing job history on a resume or application. (See Section 16.3.)

6. Always tell the truth about a criminal record on the application form and in an interview if questioned. Be prepared to show that you are rehabilitated. Contact the EEOC if you have questions about your employment rights.

7. It is never too late to reverse a bad situation by making a change. Make a plan for change that is realistic, or it will fail. Do not try to conquer the world in one week, month or year. Have a long-term goal, but approach it in steps that you will be able to accomplish. Seek mentors who will be able to help you along the way. As you accomplish each step, your confidence will build and you will be able to go the long haul and probably exceed your goal.

Chapter 15

I want to make a career change

You've had a good job with the same company for 10 years. It has provided you with a new car, a small savings account and some great friends. You have even become somewhat skilled at what you do, and, as a result, you've been promoted twice and are now one of the company's most valued employees. Everything seems perfect—except that what you're doing is not what you really want to do. You know exactly what you want to do, but you don't know how to make the change. If that scenario somewhat reflects your situation, be encouraged. There are avenues available that will get you where you want to be, and you can start from where you are right now.

15.1 I know what I want to do—but I need more education

When the software company Clara worked for as a data processing clerk was sold, everyone was told they would have three months to either relocate with the company or they would be out of a job.

"This is the pits," Clara said in frustration to her friend Katherine.

"I don't see why," Katherine replied smiling. "You don't like that job anyway."

"That's not the point. It pays the bills and I just started saving some money so that I can go to school to study fashion design. If I move to the new location, I'll be in a new environment, maybe incur more living costs and I probably won't be able to go to school."

"Okay. I know you're upset, but maybe this will turn out to be a blessing in disguise. Let's explore your options. Wouldn't it be a good idea to at least visit the new location as well as check to see if you can study design there."

"That sounds really reasonable, except it just doesn't feel good. I don't want to relocate and give up my lifestyle and be separated from my family and friends."

"Okay then. I can understand that one. How about getting a job in fashion design now? You spend practically every weekend making wedding ensembles. I think your designs are great and I bet a design house would, too."

"Thanks, Kathy. But I don't have the proper credentials or experience. I need to finish my education and then get more training before they would even look at me."

"Why don't you try to get a data processing job in the fashion industry, or do something connected with fashion. At least you would be around people you relate to, you could continue your education and who knows—you might make some contacts that will help you with your career."

"Kathy, that's a great idea. I really hadn't thought about putting it all together that way. I'm going to look into that right away."

Clara chose to develop a chronological resume that relied heavily on her data processing and administrative skills. She figured that she could get into a fashion company based on those strengths and, once in, explore some options for movement.

She used several strategies to access jobs: networking with friends; sending resumes to companies listed under the fashion section in the yellow pages; sending resumes to major department stores; and listing with two temporary agencies that specialized in placing people in the fashion industry.

During her first temp assignment, Clara discussed her designs with the employer and was told she had potential. She believed her desire for a career in fashion was a deciding factor in her being offered a permanent position. Four months after she accepted the permanent position, Clara had readjusted her lifestyle and enrolled in school.

So for Clara, what initially seemed a catastrophe turned out to be a blessing in disguise.

15.2 I know what I want to do—but I need experience

Jerry's situation was different than Clara's. He was not losing his job but still had the same compelling desire to make a career change. Jerry had worked for more than seven years in a corporate accounting department, but he wanted to be a business writer. His problem was a lack of practical experience.

He solicited advice for getting started from one of the writers in his company's public affairs department. She suggested that he volunteer his services within the company and in his professional association to gain the experience and credibility he needed. Jerry followed her advice and wrote a column for the employee newsletter, developed a procedures manual for his department's budget process and wrote some public relations material for a local professional organization. He also took some business writing classes and was able to expand his network of contacts through the people he met there.

It was 18 months after he started his volunteer writing before he got a chance to apply for a position in his company. When his friend in the public affairs department alerted him that one of the writers was leaving, Jerry assembled his portfolio and prepared a resume highlighting his writing accomplishments. As soon as the position was vacated, Jerry contacted the manager and requested an interview.

Even with his portfolio, the manager seemed a little hesitant to give Jerry the job. So Jerry suggested that he be given the position on a trial basis for three months, and if the manager was satisfied with his performance, they could talk about a permanent arrangement. The manager agreed and Jerry was on the road to a new career.

Planning, patience, volunteer assignments and compromise all worked together to help Jerry make his career change.

15.3 I know what I want to do—but there are no openings

When Jill lost her position at the bank through downsizing, she was ecstatic. "Now I finally have the opportunity to do what I want to do!" she told anyone who would listen.

Her first step was to meet with a career counselor to develop a resume and discuss strategies for moving from private industry to the nonprofit sector.

"John, I have always wanted to work in social service, but my degree is not in that area and I don't have any experience. So how do I get there from here?"

"If you've never had any experience in that area, how do you know that you want to work in social service?"

"I've never had a *paid* position in social service, but I've done a lot of volunteer work for agencies over the past three years and have even headed up some projects. I know I love doing that kind of work."

"Well then, you actually do have relevant experience. Your volunteer activities will be valuable in showing your skills as well as your motivational level and commitment. Plus, you have all those great contacts you made while implementing your projects. This change should work out really well for you."

Jill and John worked to fashion a functional resume, focusing on Jill's volunteer experience and rewording some of her financial accomplishments so they emphasized skills that were transferable to the nonprofit sector. She then scheduled several informational interviews with nonprofit agencies, networked with all her volunteer contacts and sent her resume to all the agencies within her geographic area.

Two months later, Jill still had not had a serious job interview and she was starting to feel frustrated. She sought counsel from John again.

"What kind of input did you get from your informational interviews?" John asked.

"The people I talked with were all very encouraging, but no one had an opening. 'No budget' is all I hear."

"How about another approach? Do you know what you want to do and which agency you would like to work with?"

"Sure. I even have a project in mind, but they don't have a budget either."

"Why don't you write the project up as a proposal, including a salary for you as project manager, of course, and suggest to the agency that they support your effort to get the funding. That way you would have a job you want, and they would have another viable program to administer."

"John, that's a great idea!"

The agency thought so, too. Within three months, Jill had interim funding and her project was included with those that were to be proposed for annual funding.

Jill accomplished her career change by being committed enough to her goal to gain a lot of experience through volunteer activities, networking with the professional contacts she'd made over a three-year period—and being creative in her final strategy.

15.4 You're ready for a career change when...

When your career is no longer stimulating and challenging, it's time to make a change. Values and priorities are continually changing. What is important at 20 may have changed priority by 35. Certainly after working in a profession for a number of years, it is possible to outgrow it or to acquire other skills and interests that would make another career goal more compelling.

The most difficult part of making a career change has been accomplished once you decide what you want to do. Even though your first jobs may have seemed a waste of time in relation to your new career goal, they were not. More than likely, they have provided some knowledge that will be beneficial in helping you succeed in your new career.

Ultimately, you will realize your new career goal by using some skills from your first career, except now you'll bring more skill, experience and wisdom to the job.

Resolutions

1. A significant part of the process of making a career change has already been accomplished when you've decided what you want to do.

2. If you are laid off or thrust into a situation of having to change jobs, seize the opportunity to make the career change at that time.

3. Just because you were at the top of one profession does not mean that you can change careers and still be at the top—at least not at first. Be willing to start at the bottom of your new career and work your way up.

4. Your plan for progress should include obtaining the necessary degree or specialized training, as well as pursuing positions that will provide experience for growth.

5. Be flexible and willing to explore all options and strategies to obtaining your goal.

6. If you are working, consider volunteering for projects within your department or company that will not only enhance your experience but also make hiring managers aware of your goal, commitment and capabilities.

7. Volunteer your services to organizations outside your company that would provide experience as well as excellent networking contacts.

8. Plan to use a functional resume when marketing your skills to make a career change. Include accomplishments from paid as well as volunteer activities on the resume. Get feedback on the resume's appropriateness from people who are doing what you want to do.

9. Sometimes people will offer to refer your resume to others. While this is a gracious gesture, it may not be helpful to you when making a career change. The prospective employer needs to meet you. So, suggest that you call the prospect using the name of the referral or that you follow up with the prospect after the resume has been passed on.

10. Networking is one of the most effective ways to make a career change. In the networking discussion, be prepared to communicate how your skills transfer to the new career by stressing relevant aspects of accomplishments in paid and volunteer activities.

11. Join some new organizations! A quicker way to get onto your new career path is to join some of the professional organizations appropriate to your field. As a member, you'll meet lots of new contacts who can offer information and assistance in finding job opportunities.

12. Consider temporary agencies as an avenue to get into a new company or industry that has the kind of jobs you want. Once in the company, you'll be able to network with others so you'll find out about opportunities when they open up.

13. If you find yourself unable to see options for progressing toward your goal, discuss the situation with other professionals who are doing similar work. Get suggestions from them on how they have handled a situation similar to yours.

Chapter 16

I need to relocate

There are many reasons you might choose to relocate—not the least of which is for a better job opportunity. You might be spurred on by other reasons as well—a better cost of living, higher salaries, recreational opportunities, lower crime rates, better schools, cleaner air, better weather or something as nebulous as a better quality of life. Or you may choose to relocate because you've responded to a particular job opportunity that requires a move. Whatever your reason, relocation always puts a different spin on the job search process, adding unique challenges for the job hunter to confront.

16.1 In search of better job opportunities

"I'm tired of the rat race in this town," Steve told his wife, Eileen. "And now that we're going to have a family I think it's the perfect time to leave."

"Where will we go?" Eileen asked. "What about our friends and all our plans?"

"We're going where I can make a decent living doing something I enjoy. The jobs I've had since the industry started drying up here have been very disheartening. The *real* growth now is in the Southwest. That's where we should explore.

"And the weather's so much nicer there. You know, I have relatives in Arizona and Texas. We should check with them for information about cost of living and school systems.

"And I'll check into career opportunities in the industry. I'm going to start the process tomorrow. A friend at work recommended an agency that helped someone he knows to get a job with a company that was willing to pay relocation costs. Hey, I wonder if salaries are higher there. This could be the best decision we ever made!"

Indeed, a decision to relocate can be a wise one, not only for your career, but for your lifestyle as well. As you contemplate relocating to improve your job opportunities, it's a good idea to revisit the self-assessment process and give thought to your values and life preferences, as well. If the jobs are plenty in both Denver and Seattle—your love of skiing and loathing of rain are important factors in your final decision.

In order to make the best move possible, it's important to do plenty of research ahead of time. Don't just make a decision to pull up roots because of a rumor that jobs are plenty somewhere else. They may be at a salary level that could never support you and your family. Find out as much as you can about the job market and other aspects of your prospective destination. You should be exploring the following issues:

Relocation checklist

- Are experts forecasting economic growth for the area you're considering?
- Is there growth in your particular industry?
- Are other sectors of business growing as well?
- Is there a diversity of companies in the area, or does it appear to be a one-company town?
- Are there companies of various sizes? Or are they all large—or small?
- Are the average salary ranges lower or higher than other areas of the country?
- What is the cost of living in this area, particularly housing costs?
- What is the culture of the new environment? What is the ethnic mixture, predominant age range and median socio-economic level of the population?
- What recreational avenues are available? How far to a major metropolitan area, or how far to a suburban area?
- If you have a working spouse, what opportunities are available in his or her field?
- What are the schools like?
- What is the climate and which natural disasters frequent the area?

This is a lot of information to gather, but most of it is easily obtained using a sampling of the following references at your local library:

Job guides

Encyclopedia of Associations. For job placement committees, divided by regions and state.

The Job Seeker's Guide (Gale Research). Divided by regions of the country.

The Wall Street Journal reprints employment opportunities in its *National Business Employment Weekly.*

Local newspapers for all major cities. Subscribe to the local paper of the community you're considering, so you can check real estate prices and availability, even food prices.

Salaries

American Almanac of Salaries (Avon).

Occupational Compensation Survey (Bureau of Labor Statistics).

General information and points of interest

50 Fabulous Places to Raise Your Family by Lee and Saralee Rosenberg (Career Press).

Cities of the United States (Gale Research). Several volumes divided by sections.

Encyclopedia of Associations. Several volumes divided by sections of the country. Lists regional, state and local organizations, including chambers of commerce.

Computer online references to currently published information.

Magazines for major cities.

Phone books for all areas.

Geographic economic indicators

Barron's, published weekly by *The Wall Street Journal*

Business Week

Buyouts and Acquisitions

Forbes

Fortune

Money

Nation's Business

16.2 Where to find the jobs

Now that you've researched your target destination and have confirmed this is where you want to move, it's time to zero in on the specific job opportunities that are available. You have a number of information sources. Already, you should be receiving the local papers as well as the *National Business Employment Weekly,* which identifies specific job openings and reprints jobs listed in *The Wall Street Journal.* But as you know, it's most often the unadvertised jobs that offer the best opportunities. Here are some ways to track these openings down:

- Working through an employment agency can be an excellent way to find out about jobs in a new location. If the agency is handling the position on retainer, they will have a good idea of how the management is likely to respond to relocating a new employee. Plus, if a company has already committed to paying an agency fee, it may be an indication of the value they have placed on getting the right person for the position. (Companies working with recruiting agencies are also more likely to pay relocation expenses!) The guidelines below will assist with agency selection.

- Networking with friends and professional associates is another excellent source for job information. You may find out about jobs through your contacts at a professional association that has national chapters or an alumni group.

- Your contacts, whether friends, business contacts or family, who live in your desired location may also be able to help you track down job opportunities.

- Targeting companies in the new area may provide some results. (See Section 21.1.)

16.3 Relocating with the help of an agency

It's best to work through a local agency that has an office or working arrangement with another agency in the city where you want to relocate. To help determine if the agency is reputable, call the employment office of several large companies and ask them either to recommend or give you their opinion of agencies you are considering. A listing of agencies can usually be found under "Employment" in business directories or the yellow pages.

When choosing an agency, ask if they handle your skill area. Specialization agencies handle only particular groups of jobs—

for instance, only technical positions. Using this type of agency can be an advantage. Employers learn of their concentration and turn to them for that type of candidate. Those agencies will know quite a lot about their industry. They are good barometers of what kind of salary to expect and will be in the best position to help you.

Ask if a fee is involved and, if so, who pays it. It is probably enough to just use agencies where the fee is paid by the employer.

Key points to remember when working with an agency are:

- Stay in control of your search. Insist, in writing, that the agency let you know before forwarding your resume for an opening, because it may be to a company where you have already made contact.

- Before you sign any contract, ask if you may take it home to review. If the representative says there is some reason why you can't, the agency may not be reputable and you shouldn't do business there.

- If the contract specifies a fee at both ends (registration and then finder's or location fee after they've found you a job), be careful. This might indicate the agency is collecting a fee from you and the employer.

- Agency reps don't make any money unless they make a placement. Sometimes in their zeal to do so, they will try to place you in a position you're not interested in or misrepresent your qualifications to a prospective employer. Be clear about your career goals and the type of assignments you want.

- All good reps readily admit that finding a job takes considerable work on your part. They can't do it all for you. This is one of your most important clues in identifying an ethical firm.

- Be careful about telling reps about positions you are pursuing. Once they know of an opening, they may send other applicants to compete with you.

- In addition to evaluating the agency, interview the representative you will be working with. How long has the person been a recruiter and what is his or her experience in placement? Does he or she belong to any associations or groups that will give them access to the types of jobs you'd be interested in? Does the person seem honest and credible?

Types of agencies

Agencies that deal with the employment process fall into one of the following categories:

- **Employer fee-paid agencies.** These may be search firms that handle permanent placement, temporary placement agencies or agencies that do both. The employer bears the cost of either type of placement. Search firms either work on a retainer (fee paid up front, usually for high-end positions), or a contingency (fee paid when a placement is made). Temporary agency fees are ongoing while you work for the company. If you accept a permanent job with the company while working through a temporary agency, the company owes the agency a permanent placement fee. Most agencies specialize in skills sets and will tell you if they handle yours. It is best not to list with more than two permanent placement agencies at a time in order to avoid conflict over fees if both agencies submit your resume to the same company. It is fine to list with several temporary placement agencies.

- **Employee fee-paid agencies.** These firms require either a flat fee or a percentage of your expected annual income for helping you with the job search process. Generally, that process involves only resume preparation and referral of your resume to many companies, as well as interview practice and critiques. These agencies do not get you a job; the companies to which your resume is forwarded contact you directly if they are interested in you. These agencies also require you to sign a contract promising to pay a certain sum of money. Once you've signed, you are legally obligated to pay them that sum, whether you find a job or not. Most communities have some free agencies and non-profit groups providing similar career counseling services. These may be a more reasonable alternative to an agency where you must pay a fee.

16.4 Rewriting your resume for relocation

When writing to companies outside of your area or responding to their ads (if you are willing to pay your own relocation costs or if you were planning to move anyway), it is best to show on your resume and cover letter a phone number and address in the city where you plan to relocate in order to avoid deselection. Some companies will automatically reject your application if it is outside the city, often figuring they can find someone local. During the interview you can discuss relocation, if it is appropriate. You might find that some companies will assume all or a portion of the cost of your relocation, including selling your house.

16.5 Interviewing long-distance

It is important that you maintain the professional image already established by your resume by doing the following:

- If you have elected to use a local answering service in the area to which you wish to relocate, then you should be sure that calls from prospective employers are answered in a professional manner. To avoid being unprepared when using your home phone, keep the answering machine on, and make sure your message is professional, not cutesy.

- When you return the call, have your data organized in front of you—names, numbers, your resume and the ad to which you responded, the points you'd like to make and desired results. If the interviewer is not available, set a specific "interview" time with the secretary, stressing that you will be at your number and will await his or her call.

- Follow the normal rules of interviewing, and make sure your tone of voice is positive and confident. It is helpful to maintain a smile while talking. That will help convey a positive attitude.

- When the interviewer says he or she wants you to fly out, make sure it is clear who will make the arrangements and what the arrangements include—expenses to and from the location, hotel, meals, etc.—and how they will be paid for. Try to get the interviewer to be responsible for coordinating the trip and payment.

- Be prepared to answer questions about your desire to move, such as, "What makes you think you'll be happy here?" or "How does your family feel about relocating?" (The latter inquiry, if posed to both males and females alike, would be permissible.) Employers know that a family's negative reaction to a move could ultimately cause a problem for an employee and, as a result, the company. A good reply might be, "We have done research on the area and like what we've discovered so far. Of course, I couldn't make a final decision until we've visited the location."

16.6 They offered me a job—but they want me to relocate

Peter was stunned. He didn't know whether to jump with joy or collapse in despair. The company that had been courting him for six months had finally come through with the job of his dreams— but it meant a relocation to Alaska.

"It's the chance of a lifetime," Peter told his wife. "I think we ought to at least think about it."

"I can't help being negative. What if you get there and they decide after a few months they don't like you. Then what?"

"I haven't discussed that possibility with them yet, but I will."

"And another thing. What about the house. If we move, are they willing to pay for selling the house? And by the way, what is housing like there? Wait! Don't tell me. They're running a special on igloos."

"I'm glad you have a sense of humor about this. It helps. But I don't know about the housing either. That's something else I'd have to ask about."

"You've got a lot of questions to ask."

"That's right. But can we agree to at least get all the facts and evaluate the situation so we can make an informed decision?"

"Okay. I'll agree to that. But I insist on one thing. You should get a commitment from the company that we can all take a trip there to see what it would be like before you make a commitment."

"That sounds fair to me. Let's make a list of all the questions I need to ask the company and all the factors to be considered in a move like this."

A job offer that requires relocation may cause major upheaval—not only for you, but for your family. If you're married or raising children, the lives of your spouse and kids will be affected, and they'll, no doubt, have strong opinions about the move. If you're single and have family and friends in your current location, you'll want to consider how important these connections are as a support system and social outlet.

In fact, at first your reaction as well as the reactions of your loved ones may be so negative, you may decide to reject the opportunity flat out. But if an offer that includes relocation would advance your career, it deserves fair consideration and a visit to the new job site. Lifestyle and other values are just as important as the job and should be considered when making a decision. In addition to some of the questions listed in the relocation checklist in this chapter, consider these issues when exploring a relocation opportunity:

- What is the cost of living? Is your salary adequate and reflective of your job and level in that location?

- What is the culture of the new environment within the company?

- If you have a working spouse, what accommodation is the company willing to make to assist that person in locating a position if you agree to the relocation?

- What are the alternatives to relocating your family? Could you share an apartment with someone else who is in a similar situation and then commute home on a regular basis? If so, to what extent would the company be willing to subsidize the arrangement?

- Will the company pay the cost for selling your current house, or assume the mortgage if you're unable to sell it?

- If the position does not work out, what are your alternatives? Are there other companies in the area that offer positions you could fill, or would you have to relocate again to get another job or to stay on your career track?

- If the relocation does not work out within a period of time, is the company agreeable to relocating you back to your original location?

Be sure that these questions are answered before you accept or decline the offer. Frequently, when a new job requires a move, the candidate is given a little more time to consider and accept the offer. In this case, you might ask for time to make a pilot trip to the location before committing yourself.

Making a job change that involves a relocation does not have to take on the proportions of stepping off a cliff blindfolded—if you have an idea of what to expect at the new location. Whether relocating on your own or having the pilot trip financed by a prospective employer, it's your responsibility to research the area and its potential even before going on the pilot trip and certainly before making a final decision. And if you decided to move, you should have a contingency plan if the move does not work out. With all those factors in place, you'll be able to accept the change as the great adventure it can be.

Resolutions

1. Be clear about why you are relocating and research the new location to determine if it will provide what you are looking for.

2. Involve your family in developing a list of factors that they seek or are concerned about in the new location, such as schools, recreation, crime, jobs for the spouse or housing.

3. Networking is just as important in a relocation (maybe more so) as when seeking a position where you are. Take time to get referrals to contacts in the new location. They can prove invaluable to discovering inside information about the location.

4. Consider using a search agency to locate jobs. You're more likely to get an employer to pick up relocation costs by going through an agency.

5. When responding to ads in the new location, use a local phone number and address to avoid deselection.

6. Anticipate the phone interview by using an answering machine to delay the interview until you're organized.

7. Get a clear understanding from the prospective employer about who will pay the costs associated with an interview, the specifics that can be expensed and how the process will work.

8. Before accepting an offer, be clear as to the total relocation package being offered by the company, particularly the costs of selling your current home and buying one in the new location.

Chapter 17

I don't know how to get a fair salary

You deserve to be paid fairly for the skills and experience you bring to a particular job. A major obstacle to getting that salary is not knowing the market value of your skills in your geographic area. A lack of salary knowledge may cause you to base your requirements on what you *think* you deserve or undervalue your skills because you *don't know* what you deserve.

A lot of factors go into determining a fair market wage—the level of responsibility a job carries (look at things like amount of money managed or revenue earned, size of staff reporting to or level of management reporting to) as well as the education, demonstrated skill level and years of experience. Along with these factors, geographic location can play a big role. The salary for a position in Kansas would probably not be the same as it would in Chicago or Los Angeles.

Factors like age, race or sex should have no impact on salary offered. If you know what is fair and how to negotiate for it, you are more likely to keep discussions focused away from irrelevant factors and on the job, so that you will get a fair salary. But, if you base your requirements and negotiation of what you'd like to make, what bills you have to pay or what you heard the job paid five years ago, you may be disappointed with the outcome of the salary discussion. The key to getting a fair salary is knowing what your skills are worth and knowing how to negotiate for it.

17.1 Do your homework

"What's happening with your job search?" Pat asked Joyce over lunch one afternoon.

"I had a chance to interview with that company I've been trying to get in with in Springfield, but I turned it down."

"But Joyce, do you think that was smart?"

"The salary was too low. I heard they were only offering $45,000 and that was $20,000 less than my previous salary. I'm not going to take anything less. I don't have to because I'm qualified."

"You haven't worked in five months. You can't afford to turn anything down."

Joyce may have made a big mistake by too hastily turning down an opportunity to interview because she believed the salary was too low. Of course, no one wants to make less money than they've grown accustomed to. But upon examining the situation more closely, Joyce would have discovered a number of things:

- The job was in a mid-sized Midwestern community, as opposed to Chicago where she previously earned her much higher salary.

- An incentive plan allowed employees to earn an additional $5,000 in bonuses each year, not to mention the subsidized vacations, heftier health plan and other benefits offered.

- Joyce heard a figure that was at the bottom of the salary range offered for the position. Because of her experience, she more than likely would have been offered the higher end of the $10,000 range.

We can see how quickly the wage gap closed up, once we unearthed a little more detail. It's important, then, to do some digging before you turn down a job offer, or worse, an opportunity to interview. In order to determine a fair market wage, seek out library references that indicate *current* salary ranges for your job. Also, contact friends and associates in the industry, as well as professional organizations to get a sense of equitable salary ranges.

17.2 Is the salary fair? Consider these factors

Also, be sure to consider the following factors, which will affect the salary offered:

- **Location.** Cost of living differs in different parts of the country. Teresa relocated from Los Angeles to Florida. Working through a temporary agency in both locations, she commanded a salary of $36,000 in Los Angeles and $18,000 in Florida for essentially the same job functions. But she was able to rent a large house in Florida for $500 per month, compared to the $900 she paid per month for a studio apartment in Los Angeles. Location may not be a factor when making an intercompany transfer where salary is protected.

- **Level of expertise required and offered.** Companies feel no requirement to pay you for your years of service and experience gained at another company, unless they are used in the job they offer. If as a credit manager with a staff of 10 you command a salary of $40,000, do not expect to command that same salary as a credit representative if the job description does not ask for supervisory or management experience. On the other hand, if you are hired for a position for which you are not fully qualified, but the company anticipates your gaining the experience, expect to start at a lower salary than that advertised, and don't expect a higher salary until you gain the necessary experience.

- **Benefits and special incentives.** One major company offers salaries that are a little lower than its competitors but also offers its employees international travel opportunities several times a year to desirable locations such as Barbados, Paris and Switzerland. Additionally, the employees work only four days a week. Some companies close their offices at certain times of the year, providing predictable time off in addition to regular vacations and holidays. Health and dental care, wholesale and discount opportunities, health club memberships, cars and even relocation and generous severance packages should be considered.

- **Secondary and cost-saving factors.** Consider all factors that may also have an impact on income as a result of increased cash flow. For instance, paid parking, gas savings resulting from a shorter commute or a relaxed dress code, which saves on pantyhose or suit dry cleaning bills.

17.3 A salary cut may be imminent when...

Ernest worked in the banking industry for 27 years. For 19 of those years he was a third-shift supervisor in the data management unit. During that time he became accustomed to the nice lifestyle his $56,000 salary supported.

After interviewing with five prospective employers for positions similar to his former job, he was shocked to find that the starting salary on all those positions ranged between $27,000 and $30,000. He told the last employer he couldn't afford to work for that rate.

Eventually, Ernest realized that he would have to accept what his skills would bring on the market. No employer was going to pay him twice as much as everyone else for the same job.

Consider that if you have worked for the same employer for a number of years, your salary may be at the maximum level of the salary range for your skills. Employers do not pay for seniority gained at another company. They're only willing to pay market value for your skills.

Another reason your former salary might be totally outside the range of most companies is that you might be coming out of a high-paying industry, like oil or aerospace. In those instances, your choices are to adjust your living standard or relocate to a geographic area that may be able to support your salary requirements. Salary ranges are calculated based on geographic location, skills and supply and demand. (See Chapter 16.)

If employers know that you're coming out of a high-paying industry, they may be reluctant to consider you if your former salary was a lot higher than their range. If you know in advance this is the case, be prepared to explain that your former salary was appropriate for that company and industry, that the right position is the most important consideration for you and that you expect to receive a salary that is appropriate for that position and industry. If you've done your research, you should be able to indicate what salary range you believe to be appropriate.

17.4 Revealing salary information: When is the right time?

Now that you're convinced *not* to turn down an opportunity to pursue a job because the initial salary range may not be what you're looking for, you've got to work on keeping the prospective employer from turning *you* down, because your salary history or requirements may not match the job offer. Often, when a candidate reveals this information in a cover letter or initial phone interview, the employer immediately scratches him or her off the interview list because the salary needs appear too high—or even too low. (Employers may fear they cannot keep a candidate who has a high salary requirement or that the candidate is underqualified if he or she expects too little.)

Your goal is to land the interview and convince the employer that you're the best match for the job. Once you've done this, *then* you can haggle over salary. Bringing up the salary issue too soon in the game may put you out of the contest.

It took weeks after the time Brad's company laid off its manufacturing force before he was finally able to land a job interview. Although he was clearly qualified for the positions he'd applied for, he wasn't getting any return calls. So he was quite relieved when a large company asked him in for an interview. Even though he'd been with a smaller operation, his position encompassed more facets than the position for which he was being considered, so he felt very qualified to handle the interview.

The employer seemed pleased with him—until they started discussing salary. He told the employer he wanted to at least maintain his salary of $65,000. Shortly after that, the interviewer concluded the interview, shook Brad's hand and said good-bye.

It was clear to Brad that something had gone wrong in the interview and that he had lost the opportunity. What Brad did not know was that the employer had a tag of $80,000 on the position. The employer assumed that Brad must not be qualified for the job as he had originally thought. Brad's experience was devalued because of his low salary requirements. After all, the employer was looking for an $80,000-a-year-person.

What mistakes did Brad make in his job search efforts? First, he didn't do the research on salary that he should have. If he had, he may have known that the job he was applying for carried a higher price tag than he'd had before.

Secondly, he was too forthcoming in sharing his exact salary information with prospective employers at the wrong time. By knowing and quoting an appropriate *range*, which would encompass his former salary, rather than an *exact* salary, he could leave the door open for discussion. For instance, "My salary was in the range of $65,000 to $80,000." Lastly, he wasn't even considered for a number of interviews, because he responded to the requests from the classified ads by offering them his salary history and requirements up front in the cover letters that accompanied his resume. These companies either found his salary needs to be too high or too low and cut him from the running.

17.5 Responding to salary information requests in ads and applications

Some ads will request salary history and some will say the resume will not be considered without salary history. It is generally not true that resumes of qualified applicants are not considered for not including salary information. But in those instances where you feel compelled to respond, it is best to indicate a salary range that you would consider rather than a specific salary history. Offer as broad a range as possible; something like, "Seeking a salary range of $35,000 to $45,000, based on industry standards."

The biggest problem with including salary in a cover letter is that if the range you quote does not fall within the guidelines the employer has set for the position, you may not be considered. It is best to say in the letter that salary is open or negotiable and will be based upon the job requirements.

These suggestions also apply to application forms. While you may feel compelled to include salary history and requirements, fearing elimination if you don't, you are not required to do so. You can write "will discuss" in those sections requesting salary history and "open" or "negotiable" in the section requesting salary requirements.

When you sign the application form, that constitutes written permission to contact your former employers to verify any information. So if you give a range, the former employer can only attest to whether your salary fell within that range. The range you give does not have to be the exact range that represented your former position. It can be the range you develop as a result of your research—as long as your actual salary falls somewhere within that range.

17.6 Responding to salary information requests during the interview

It's best, however, not to reveal your hand until you know exactly what the employer is planning to offer. And you'll usually not know this until the interview stage. If you are confronted with the salary question early on in the interview, try to put it off, responding something like, "Oh, I'm sure we can come to an agreeable salary. But first, I'd like to know a little more about the position and whether we feel it's a good match." If you're pressed for your requirements, give a range that falls within the industry standard, and try to move on.

Had Brad known what the fair market value of the position was, he could have responded to his interviewer by saying, "I understand that the industry standard for such a position is around $75,000 to $85,000, and that seems appropriate to me."

Here is how a discussion about salary might follow:

> **Interviewer:** "Before I can pass your information along for consideration, Mary, I would need to have some idea of the salary you're seeking."

Mary: "It would really depend on the job. I'm open, but I understand that this type of position is starting between $48,000 and $55,000. How does that fit with the budget you have for the position?"

Notice that Mary gave an industry standard and still did not lock herself into an actual salary. And in both instances she turned the question right back to the interviewer to find out what salary range was set for the position.

Suppose the interviewer had asked Mary how she came up with that range. Mary could comfortably say that she had done some research to make sure her expectations were in line with the market standard and that she had obtained that information by talking with several companies.

The purpose for giving an industry range is to get past the initial levels of the interview process, get through the interview and get an offer. *Then* you are in a position to negotiate salary!

17.7 Negotiate your salary like a pro

Congratulations! You got the offer! All your hard work and perseverance have paid off—and they *want* you. So what if the salary isn't exactly what you had in mind? In this market, you can't afford to be choosy, right?

Not necessarily. When you are selected out of a pool of candidates, it is because you have been determined to be the best choice. Because of that, you have some room for negotiation after an offer has been made. Consider the following before responding to an offer:

Delay your response. It is perfectly acceptable to ask for a couple of days to consider an offer before responding. Usually, employers expect candidates to ask for some time—generally no more than a day or so. If the company demands an immediate response, you may want to consider if this is the right employer.

At the time of the offer, though, if you think it is a job that you will want to accept, let the interviewer know that right away but leave yourself an opening for further negotiation. For example:

"This sounds like a wonderful opportunity. Could I have a couple of days to review everything and get back to you Thursday morning with my acceptance?"

This approach puts you in a win-win position with the interviewer. At this point, he or she knows that you want the position and believes that an acceptance will be forthcoming.

If the offer is in the form of a letter, it's even easier to prepare for negotiation because you don't have to respond until you're ready to negotiate.

Consider the whole package. At the time you receive the offer, you should be given all the information regarding your compensation plan, including salary, vacation and sick-day policies, health benefits, incentive programs, profit-sharing and pension plans and more. You should weigh all these factors in your decision. For example, while your salary might not be as high as you would have liked, you may discover that your health plan covers dental and eye care—and to a family in braces and glasses, this could be a significant financial plus! Or you may find that you receive an extra week of vacation each year.

Evaluate the compensation package, and consider the other factors listed in Section 17.3. If, after evaluation, you believe the salary and benefits are appropriate for the position and you are satisfied with the package, then accept it.

Is the compensation package fair? When your research shows that the salary is below the industry standard for the responsibilities and the other benefits don't make up for this, then you should negotiate for a more equitable package. The discussion should center around equitable pay for the responsibilities.

Do your skills match the job advertised? If the salary being offered is in line with the industry rate for that position, then there is no valid basis for negotiating a higher salary. Your former salary and personal need are not a basis for negotiation. If you are interested in expanding the benefits segment of the compensation package, then those are the only items that need to be discussed.

Do your skills exceed the ones advertised for the job— and will they be used? Evaluate what is being asked of you in the position. Will the employer be utilizing skills not listed as part of the published advertisement for the position? For instance, the ad asked for an analyst. You have that capacity plus supervisory experience that the employer now indicates will be used in a lead capacity. In that case, you have a legitimate basis for negotiating a higher salary.

First, clarify with the employer the responsibilities of the position and agree on the "redefinition" of the job that was advertised. Next, point out the industry standard for the redefined position and suggest to the interviewer that the salary be raised. For instance:

"The position is really ideal but, based on my research, the salary seems a little low for skills that will be used and the

responsibilities. The standard seems to be around $45,000 for this type of responsibility. How does that fit with your budget?"

If there is a possibility of a higher salary, the interviewer may be open to an increase based on your discussion and may indicate that he or she will look into the matter and get back with you. If a higher salary is not possible, the interviewer will usually say so. In that case, suggest that you table that discussion until a later date— say, in about three months—at which time you believe you will have demonstrated value worth the compensation you've requested.

How to handle some common negotiation situations

1. When you know you want (or need) the job and will take it even if the salary is not changed, go for a win-win approach.

Say: *"I'm excited about this position and the possibility of being a part of your team, but, according to my research, the salary is below the industry standard. Would your budget permit $45,000 instead of $40,000, which I believe would bring it in line?"* By referring to the budget, you won't put the employer on the spot.

Don't say: *"I'd like to have this job, but my wife (or husband) and I have discussed it, and we can't pay our house note on that salary."* Your house note is your own responsibility and not that of the employer.

2. When the employer says the salary is locked in for some reason—cost-cutting effort, time for you to prove yourself, limited budgets—acknowledge the negative, address it with a positive, then offer alternatives.

Say: *"I certainly understand the need to maintain a reasonable budget, but I feel confident that the skills I'll be able to demonstrate within a relatively short period of time are worth the additional compensation. Could we agree to a performance review in three months and another discussion about salary at that time?"* This will give you time to make yourself valuable to the employer and determine if there are any obstacles to overcome in gaining a salary increase. (Be sure to get this in an offer letter or put it in your final acceptance letter.)

Don't say: *"I don't think the salary is enough. Can you see if you can get me more?"* This approach may create a negative situation for you and the employer because it offers no way out. If the employer can't get more, it will make him or her uncomfortable knowing that if you accept, you will have done so grudgingly and you will probably continue to look for another position.

3. When the employer says the decision is not made by him or her but by personnel.

Say: *"I understand, but before I discuss it with personnel, I'd like to just run it by you first to determine if my request is in line."* Sometimes deferring to personnel is a tactic to avoid having the salary discussion. Whether the decision is made by personnel or not, the salary comes out of the manager's budget, so the manager is likely to have some input in the final decision. So try to get concurrence on your approach to personnel.

Don't say: *"Could you check with them about getting me more?"* It would then be easy for the manager to say, *"I checked and it was no-go,"* which would force you to end the discussion right there, without alternatives.

4. When the salary is quite a bit out of line with the market, the manager will entertain no alternatives, and you have no compelling reason to accept the decision (like the rent is due next week), then you may want to refuse the offer, but keep the contact.

Say: *"Although I understand your budget limitations, I believe it would be unfair to both of us for me to accept a position I couldn't commit to. I would like to stress, though, that I think we would work well together, and I do like the company. So if another position should come up with a salary more in line with the market, I hope that you will consider me."* Emphasis should be placed on "liking the person," in order to maintain a good networking contact.

Don't say: *"Well, I'm sorry. That salary is ridiculous* (even if you think it is), *and I couldn't possibly work for that."*

Getting a fair salary for your skills is up to you. Don't expect employers to be responsible for keeping your best interests in mind. Employing you is part of getting a service they need to carry out their business. It makes good business sense for the employer to get that service for the most economical price possible. And it makes good business sense for you to know the value of that service and be willing to negotiate, if necessary, to get it.

Resolutions

1. Know the industry standard for your skills in your geographic location.

2. Accept that salaries differ by location and that the employer is not paying you for your seniority at another company but, rather, for the experience you will actually use at his or her company.

3. Develop a salary range for your skills by checking with friends, associates and references available in the library.

4. Instead of quoting an actual salary in cover letters, on applications and in interviews, quote a salary range that includes your former salary.

5. Be prepared to negotiate salary—after the offer—if it is below the industry standard.

6. Salary negotiations should be based on the job's responsibilities and market value, not on personal considerations.

7. Enter into any salary or job negotiation with a win-win attitude by approaching the meeting with an open mind and with alternatives for achieving appropriate compensation.

Chapter 18

I don't know whether to accept the offer

Congratulations! After all your hard work, you landed an offer! Go ahead, pat yourself on the back. You deserve it. But before you jump with joy and eagerly promise your prospective employer that you'll be dedicated to working for him or her forever, stop. Take a deep breath. And follow these steps before you give your acceptance.

18.1 Ask for time to consider the offer

While you may be pressured to give an immediate answer, it is an accepted business practice to allow a job candidate time to consider the offer. This can range anywhere from 24 hours or over the weekend, to as much as two weeks for higher-paying executive positions. Whatever your circumstances, you *should* take the time to give the offer the serious consideration it deserves. Even if you're *positive* you'll accept the job.

You might respond to the good news with something like this: "I'm pleased and excited to be offered this opportunity. I feel very positive about working with you, but I would like some time to consider the offer carefully. Could I call you back with my acceptance on Monday morning?"

What works with this approach is that you are positive and indicate you *want* to work for the company. You've also identified the course of action and indicated exactly when you'll contact the employer with your answer. So now, what is it that you have to "carefully consider" before you call back with your response?

18.2 Make sure you know what you've been offered

You might be so excited at the prospect of having a job again that you haven't paid much attention to what it is you've been offered. While you've probably clarified the job responsibilities and know what your title would be, you need to consider the following: How about other particulars? When do you start? What are your hours? What about benefits, vacation time? Who do you report to? What—and how—will you be paid? All these issues may have been discussed at one time or another during your interview. But to make sure you and your employer are both in synch with what the offer entails, make sure these details are spelled out clearly. What's the best way to do that? Read the following section.

18.3 Get the offer in writing

Frequently, employers will automatically put the job offer in a formal letter, for their own protection as much as for the employee. It's crucial that you have something in writing in order to protect yourself from unpleasant and often devastating surprises—such as, while you're considering the offer and perhaps turning down other offers, the employer withdraws the offer.

If it appears the company does not intend to put the offer in writing and you're uncomfortable about making this demand, you can still protect yourself by drafting a letter outlining what you understand to be the terms of the offer. Include all information about title, salary, supervisor, benefits, start date and hours, and request that the employer confirm whether your understanding is correct. Don't respond with an answer until you have this confirmation.

18.4 Negotiate the offer

If necessary, you may have to negotiate some specific terms of the offer, such as salary, hours, promotions, reviews or specific benefits. Examine the package thoroughly and in its entirety before you get upset and make an issue of, say, the fact that you have to pay for parking. If you need to make some adjustments, now is the time to bring up those issues. For a further discussion of salary negotiation, please review Chapter 17.

18.5 When you're interviewing with more than one company

The complications that occur when interviewing with several companies at a time can often cause some concern for job hunters. But whether you're juggling interviews or stalling on offers to get the one you want, you can manage this process.

Brian had four interviews over a six-week period with the chemical company he was interested in working for. At the end of the fourth interview, the prospective employer said, "Brian, it looks like we're in agreement about the important aspects of the position. As far as I'm concerned, the job is yours. When can you start?"

Brian felt his stomach lurch. While this was certainly good news, he was scheduled to interview with another company he believed might offer better opportunities than this one. While he didn't want to lose the chance for this job, he wanted to keep his options open—at least for another few days until he could gauge the results of the upcoming interview.

During your interviews you should always mention that you are "exploring possibilities." This sets the stage for you to ask for a delay in responding. Thus, "I am extremely interested in your offer and the company, but as previously mentioned, I am awaiting the outcome of other interviews. Therefore, I would like to defer my decision until _____." Give a specific date. Don't offer any details about your other possibilities. Almost without exception the company will respond in a positive manner if your request is reasonable.

You may not get an offer from the other company, so don't lose a good opportunity by playing a waiting game. If you have a solid offer on the table and are waiting to hear from another interview, put the pressure on the other company. Say something like. "I've got a solid offer from another company, and unless you can make me an offer within 24 hours, I have to accept the one on the table."

Marie was fortunate enough to receive two offers almost simultaneously. While she preferred the work environment and career direction the first company offered, she was disappointed in the salary, which was a few thousand dollars lower than the one the second company offered. Instead of passing on this opportunity and accepting the higher salaried job, or accepting the lower pay and feeling resentful, Marie confronted her prospective employer. Her discussion went something like this:

"As I had told you early in the interviewing process, I have been considering other opportunities. It turned out that I received another offer at the same time I received yours—at a salary level $5,000 higher. As much as I enjoy the energy and enthusiasm and the opportunity to advance within your company, it's difficult for me to say 'no' to a similar opportunity with more money. Is there a way you could meet this salary level?"

In most cases, employers will appreciate your honesty and also realize that if another company has extended an offer—one that surpasses theirs—their hunch is right that you're too valuable to let get away. And if not? You've got another job waiting for you!

When faced with a situation such as this, you can see why it's valuable to ask for a little time to consider the offer. This buys you the time needed to renegotiate offers if necessary. Following the negotiation meeting, send the employer an acceptance letter and list all the items agreed to.

18.6 Accepting the offer

Once you've come to an agreement regarding negotiations, or confirmed the terms of the offer in writing, you're ready to officially accept the offer.

Make a phone call. You should contact either the hiring supervisor or personnel staff who handled the interviewing process. Be sure to express your enthusiasm and pleasure at the opportunity to work with the company.

Follow up with a letter. Send the employer an acceptance letter reiterating all the details of the offer. The acceptance letter will help to keep your agreement valid should the manager for the position change before all the terms of the agreement have been fulfilled. A sample acceptance letter is found at the end of this chapter.

Finally, before you rest easy and assume you have nothing to worry about until your first day, be sure you stay on top of the follow-up. Are you required to have a physical? Take some tests? Fill out paperwork? Sign up for the company softball team? Attend the annual picnic, even before you start work? Be sure you're as diligent in following up with all of these efforts as you were in presenting yourself during the interview. You want to start your first day with your new employer perceiving you as a reliable addition to the staff.

Resolutions

1. Don't be pressured into accepting an offer on the spot—even if you know you want the job. Ask for time to consider—24 hours at the minimum.

2. Before accepting, make sure you know exactly what you've been offered—job title, pay and benefits, who you're reporting to, advancement opportunities and start date.

3. Ask for the offer in writing. Or put the offer in writing and ask the employer to confirm your understanding of the offer.

4. If there are terms you'd like to change, now's the time to negotiate them.

5. If you're interviewing with more than one company—and you receive an offer from one but want to hold out for the second, be honest. You should have made it clear to the employers initially that you were considering other opportunities. Tell the employer who makes the offer that you need some time to consider. Then alert the other employer that you've received an offer and must make a decision soon.

6. When accepting an offer, call first, then follow up with a letter.

Acceptance letter

Date

Mr. William Hart
Vice President, Operations
CBS Industries
1630 Central Avenue
Los Angeles, CA 90071

Dear Bill:

Thank you for the faith shown in me as reflected in your offer of the Manager, Administration position.

It is my understanding that the job reports to you and is responsible for legal, data processing and administrative services.

The employment package includes:

- Annual compensation of $60,000
- Stock options (based on performance)
- Key executive insurance program
- All relocation costs including purchase and sale costs of housing and mortgage assistance

I look forward to starting with the company on October 2, 1995.

Sincerely,

John Thomas

John Thomas

Chapter 19

I want an alternative to 9-to-5

Since you are currently at this crossroads of your career, why not take some time to consider alternatives that might give you more flexibility, more control, more fulfillment? Precisely because of the upheaval that's caused so much change in the work force, the job market also offers many more alternatives to workers today. Downsizing and outsourcing of corporations have resulted in a greater need for freelancers, independent contractors and consultants to help. And even those who continue to be employed by companies find that there may be more flexible job arrangements—telecommuting, part-time work, job sharing. Some workers have even made a career of temporary employment. One of the following examples may stimulate an idea of an alternative career that might fill your overall needs better.

19.1 Home-based business

At age 43, Marjorie had mixed feelings about being laid off from the company where she had worked for more than 20 years. On the one hand, it was a relief, but she had some anxiety about her next move. Should she take the opportunity to completely change her lifestyle and do something she had always wanted to do, like focus on her artwork? Or get a similar job?

Her age, the company's severance package and the fact that she had no personal obligations were all positive factors that helped her make her decision. She decided it was time to live the lifestyle she'd always dreamed of, because she might never get another chance like this. Marjorie decided to retire her gray suit, redesign one of the rooms in her home into a studio and pursue a career as an artist. She recognized it would take time to generate an income with her artwork and, even then, probably not a large one. Not wanting to deplete her resources, she got a part-time job at an art store two days a week to supplement her income. That left the rest of her time for her artwork and social life.

The organizational and administrative skills Marjorie had mastered in the business lay dormant for only 18 months. During that time, Marjorie worked at her art until she was ready for her first show, then her business skills aided her in securing a site and organizing her first show. She sold several pieces and was even contracted to do a special piece. She was making less money, but she felt a greater sense of satisfaction than ever before.

Having your own home-based business can provide a great degree of creative satisfaction, but it may not provide the type of income you'd like—even with a modified lifestyle. A part-time job can be an excellent support to the business because it provides a supplemental income. After working in a high-stress business environment, you are not likely to miss the production demands and the politics, but you might miss the structure, feedback and support provided by others. A part-time job can also help meet that need for social interaction.

When evaluating the decision, consider your personal and financial needs and obligations, how much money you'll need for the business and the revenue you expect the business to generate, how long it will take for the business to be productive and the business limitations and drawbacks.

Network with others who have a home-based business, especially in the same field. Sources for networking would be classes (students and teachers), suppliers of products or services to the small business owners and professional associations for home-based business owners.

19.2 Telecommuting—a logical move

Gloria worked 13 years for a mid-sized management consulting firm before deciding to make a career change.

Even though she experienced significant personal trauma in her life during the 13-year period, she was able to manage those obstacles and still maintain her career.

She began to feel stagnant in her job around the same time her company started some cutbacks. Since she didn't see any opportunity for growth or change coming out of the restructuring, she decided to seek a another job opportunity.

Having tired of the corporate environment, but still desiring some of the benefits of being associated with a company, she decided to look for a telecommuting opportunity. Through her contacts, she lined up and negotiated a contract with one company for a limited number of hours per week and partial benefits. The contract, her fax, computer, e-mail and teleconferencing enabled her to work at home and only commute to the company's East Coast location six or seven times a year.

Working from home allowed her to do some part-time consulting and offered the added benefit of being able to let the plumber in while she was working. The job, in combination with the consulting, gave her the variety, stimulation and freedom she needed.

Working from home or starting a business is an option that 25 percent of new job changers choose to explore. It has obvious benefits of freedom and flexibility, but it requires tremendous self-discipline and the ability to work effectively without feedback. The downside can be the feeling of isolation, inadequate equipment or supplies, duplication of effort in the face of poor coordination and not knowing when the day is over—working past the normal time you would in an office.

19.3 Freelancing

Lee had achieved a successful 20-year career with a Fortune 100 company as a graphics designer by the time he got the opportunity to retire early. With his children married and with the modest income from his wife's small costume jewelry shop, he had no real money worries. But after being a productive worker for such a long time he was quickly bored with the amount of time he had on his hands.

He shared his feelings with one of his former co-workers, who suggested that he do some freelance work for the company. His work had been well regarded and there was certainly a need. Lee followed up on the suggestion and got an assignment immediately. By using his contacts and the references from the assignments at his former company, he was able to get assignments with several other companies.

It wasn't long before he had more work than he could handle and actually had to refuse assignments. It didn't take him long to set a schedule for himself that involved work, helping his wife in the shop and leisure activities. For him, freelancing was the perfect compromise to total retirement.

Freelancing can provide a wonderful opportunity to keep your foot in a productive environment. Some assignments may be at a company location and some may allow working at home, which also provides some variety. It's wise to consider that if freelancing is your main source of income, you must be committed to developing more than one client, no matter how lucrative that client is. If you don't, and the client's situation changes suddenly, you'll be left with no income for some time.

19.4 Working as a "temp"

When Ellen's company closed down her division, she was left with 18 years of secretarial experience and a desire to do something she really wanted to do while at the same time make good money. She wanted something with variety, maybe a little excitement, new people and new situations—except she didn't know what that something would be.

A suggestion from a friend set her on the right track. Her friend suggested a career in hotel management or the entertainment fields. Ellen decided that she would like to try both those areas and maybe others. She signed up with a couple of temporary agencies to access a variety of fields, and it turned out to be the perfect solution. She was able to make a decent income and experience the variety she wanted without having to make a commitment to a particular industry. And whenever she decided—if she ever did—that she wanted to pursue a career in a particular area, she could then start looking for a permanent job.

"Temping" has the big advantage of putting you in a variety of places, allowing you to meet a lot of people and gather new experiences. For some, the lack of benefits is a negative, but some agencies have counteracted that with partial benefits programs. Temping might be the perfect alternative if your main objective is variety.

19.5 Independent contracting

After 15 years as a personnel administrator in a corporate environment, Barbara wanted out of the pressure and the politics. She quit her job because she wanted to live a more restful and relaxed life. She mainly wanted to have "regular" hours of 9 to 5, instead of the 10- and 12-hour days she had with her former employer. Her primary goal for her next job was to be able to "turn the job off" and leave it completely behind when she left work.

An old friend provided the solution. She introduced Barbara to a company that provided contract recruiters to mid-sized companies recovering and shoring up after a restructure. It was perfect for Barbara. She was able to choose the assignments she wanted and, in some instances, negotiate working days and hours. For her, the best part was using skills she already had, being able to go home on time and not having to get involved with the politics of the company.

Contracting may be a viable source for using talents you already have, especially in a corporate setting, because more and more companies are relying on outsourcing as a way of handling their staffing needs. The company you left might even call you to come back and handle your old job as a contractor! One of the obvious advantages to contracting is being on site, without having to be totally involved.

19.6 Consulting

Mitchell decided to make a big job change, and consulting as a Macintosh specialist seemed to be the best avenue for him. He believed consulting would allow him to increase his involvement in a number of community activities he enjoyed and also schedule four or five major trips per year with friends.

Three years before leaving his company, Mitchell started preparing to be a consultant by contracting his services to executives and setting up personal computer systems in their homes. He had gained such a positive reputation before he retired that his regular job, coupled with his consulting, had been almost more work than he could handle. But he had accepted the work because he knew those references would prove valuable.

His business plan included targeting college students as his primary market group and offering them a discounted service rate. He developed a flyer for distribution at the local colleges.

With his finances set, a stable social life, excellent references and referrals, and a marketing plan, he was on his way.

Alternatives to consulting would be job sharing, flextime and part-time work. These choices would afford lesser freedom than consulting because they generally require some regular hours. But the advantages could also include partial benefits, consistent income and not needing to market your services. These opportunities may be available with your former company or through a temporary placement agency.

The career alternative that's best for you will depend on a number of important factors, your age and financial needs, as well as your interests and values. The ones suggested in this chapter are primarily a compromise between working for someone, owning a full-time demanding business or not working at all. Their focus is more on adding value to your life. Nonetheless, if you are going to put your time and energy into an endeavor, it is good for your effort to be profitable, if for no other reason than as a measurement of your accomplishment.

Resolutions

1. Alternative career routes are a departure from the norm and, as such, require the extra initiative, faith and discipline of an entrepreneur.

2. Insufficient pay, boredom, perceived lack of opportunity within the company combined with a strong desire for creative control are all factors expressed by a large number of entrepreneurs. If you are experiencing these feelings, they may be leading you to consider an alternative career.

3. Leave a favorable impression with your last company, so that it will be your option to provide consulting or contracting services to them if the opportunity arises.

4. As an independent worker, you will need to keep abreast of your field, continually educating yourself in order to stay competitive.

5. Working without structure may require you to be disciplined enough to independently maintain a regular routine, be energetic and work long hours.

6. Working without the security of a stable cash flow or work flow requires you to manage periods of no activity and no money *and* periods of extreme activity and lots of money.

7. If you are seriously thinking about starting your own business, even though home-based, get help in writing a business plan. Help is available from many sources, like the chamber of commerce (which may provide a listing of community agencies), the Small Business Administration or a representative from your local bank.

Chapter 20

I haven't found a job yet

Nothing comes until you are ready—and if you are at this juncture of change in your career, you're ready for the change even if it seems that this last step will require making an Olympian effort. It's that very effort of overcoming this last obstacle that will propel you into accomplishing your goal. So if you're stuck and feeling that you've done everything you can, relax a moment, take a deep breath, and then reconsider your whole plan and approach. Discuss it with a few people you respect, make the corrections or take the new turns you need to, and move forward to accomplish your goal. The following ideas may stimulate you to get over this final hump.

20.1 Turn rejections into learning experiences

Through her networking contacts, Sandy was referred to two positions for customer service representative. She was hopeful of positive consideration from both and was extremely disappointed when other candidates were selected.

"Maybe I should just give up," she told Mary, one of the contacts. "I thought that networking into an interview would give me an inside edge on the competition."

"Networking may give you an inside edge on getting an interview, but you still have to sell yourself in that interview."

"Would you check with the interviewer and let me know where I came up short?"

"I'll be glad to do that for you."

Mary got back to Sandy the next day with feedback that the interviewer thought her communication skills fell short. "He said that you didn't project confidence when he called you for the interview, nor during the interview. He thought you were a nice person, but you seemed hesitant about your skills during the interview. He said you need to sell yourself more."

Sandy's other networking contact gave similar feedback. That contact mentioned that the employer interpreted Sandy's anxious communication during the interview as a lack of confidence.

After the feedback, Sandy realized that her problem was not her resume, which was getting her interviews; it was her poor interviewing skills. Sandy set up several practice interviews with customer services professionals, and when she was confident that she would be able to sell herself in an interview, she applied for another position—and got it.

If you're turned down for a job, follow up to learn why. If you don't have a contact who can ask for you, take a chance and call the employer directly. You may be surprised at how willing and helpful he or she may be.

20.2 Make changes!

If you learn that you lack a specific skill and that's why you're not getting the offers, take the hint! Take a class, hire a teacher or gather the experience you need.

When Ann left a high-paying position as a senior marketing secretary to relocate with her husband, she was not concerned about her ability to get a new job. After the relocation, they started their family, and Ann stayed home with her daughter until she started school. When finances necessitated that she return to work, Ann found it was not as easy as she thought.

Everyone said the same thing: "Your qualifications look great, but we need someone with computer skills."

Ann immediately enrolled in the local high school's adult education evening classes to learn computer skills. She was able to complete the three-month introductory class in six weeks. She immediately notified the temporary agencies and was placed on a temporary assignment the following week. She also notified the companies that had rejected her and let them know of her updated skills and availability.

Computer skills are easily obtained through high schools and community colleges, and usually for only a very small fee. In addition to technical skills, if you are lacking in administrative experience for the type of job you seek, consider doing some volunteer work for a high school or social service agencies. This will provide accomplishments that can be added to your resume and expand your network of contacts, which may even lead to a job.

20.3 Widen your net

If you're not making contacts or getting leads that are landing you jobs, then you need to widen your circle of contacts. Join different groups, reach out, be creative—for example, try turning some of those employers who didn't hire you into networking contacts.

After his third interview failed to produce a job offer, Jason decided he had nothing to lose—and possibly something to gain—by seeking feedback from the interviewer.

"Bob, I'd like to say again that I appreciate the interview," Jason said. "I enjoyed meeting you, and I wish you the best with the job we discussed. Because we did spend some time talking, it would helpful to me if you could give me some feedback on where else my skills might be valuable."

"I'd be happy to," Bob replied. Bob then proceeded to relate which companies he thought would benefit from Jason's experience. He also pointed out some qualities he thought Jason needed to emphasize and suggested contacts at the companies he had mentioned. And, at Jason's request, he agreed to let him use his name as the referral source when he contacted the companies.

Jason turned a rejection into a good networking contact and was able to get some objective feedback on how his skills fit in the market.

In addition to turning rejections into networking contacts, as Jason did, consider joining some different groups. Some employment development offices allow professionals to run clubs at their location. Check with your local Employment Development Department (commonly known as the unemployment office) to see if there is one you could join. If you live in a large area, there may be several of these clubs you could join. Chamber of commerce auxiliary groups may also be a good source for contacts, and the chambers may know of other groups you could join. The name of the game is to meet as many people as possible, because you never know who might be a link to your next job.

20.4 Ask your contacts, friends and co-workers for advice

"I'm getting called for jobs," Joyce said in frustration to her friend Andrea. "They're just not the jobs I want. Ever since I relocated to this town, every management job I've applied for has resulted in a call to interview for a secretarial position. I don't get it."

"Well, at least you're getting called. Let's look at your resume. Maybe it's the problem." Andrea spotted the problem after a glance at Joyce's resume. "You've got significant management and supervisory experience here, but it shows your last position was as an executive secretary. Why is that?"

"That was a temporary position that I took when I relocated here. I took it as a stop-gap measure to make some money while I looked around and assessed the job market."

"You should delete it from your resume. To an employer that is a red flag. They may think you took a secretarial job because you could not cope with the responsibilities or stress of a management job. So now we know why they've been calling you for secretarial jobs. They probably think they'd get someone more qualified than the average secretary."

Joyce made the change to her resume and, shortly afterward, started receiving calls to interview for administrative management positions.

If you're not sure what you're doing wrong in the job hunt process, ask your contacts and friends for advice. Their objective eyes may catch something you're "too close" to see.

20.5 Go to the experts

If you are continuing to struggle with the job search, consider getting the help of a resume-writer, career counselor or employment service. Sometimes, the help of a professional is all you need to boost your search in a positive direction.

After 20 years with the same company, Carol was forced to make a job change but was afraid to start the process.

She felt overwhelmed by all the job search books and was unsure of which techniques to apply to her situation. Plus, she was just scared to death to compete. So she decided to seek help from one of the career counseling services she'd seen advertised in the newspapers.

The counselor helped Carol analyze her work history, decide on industries where her skills would be a good fit and then fashion a resume for responding to ads and listing with agencies. She also gave her some advice on her wardrobe and recommended several stores where she could purchase up-to-date interview attire.

The counselor sent her to two other associates for practice interviews. Following the feedback from the interviews, they developed responses she could use in real job interviews, and then the counselor helped her to develop strategies for getting a new job. Within four weeks, Carol had two job offers. The counselor helped her to evaluate which would fit her goal best, and Carol was on her way.

For Carol, the counselor's fee was well worth it, because she needed the guidance as well as the psychological support during each step of the process.

There are many nonprofit and community organizations that offer job hunting workshops, seminars, counseling and services if you need professional support. But if you are truly having trouble even getting started and are paralyzed by the idea of the process, you may want the individual service offered by a professional career counselor.

Check in your local newspaper, in the yellow pages under employment, with friends and with personnel representatives of your former company for the names of reputable counselors.

20.6 Don't be too hard on yourself

Remember that there are former top executives and highly accomplished professionals out there who have been struggling for months—and longer—to find a job. Don't let this news concern you further, but take it as a sign that there's nothing wrong with *you*! And whatever you do, don't take rejection personally. Consider these efforts:

Every workday for 30 days, Pat checked for openings at the hospital personnel office where she was interested in working. At the end of that time, she got the first administrative opening that was available.

Lee mailed her resume every week to the same 10 companies for two months. Eventually, she got an interview and landed a position as a financial analyst with one of the companies.

Steven had a conversation with a person standing in line with him at the supermarket who turned out to be an excellent contact who helped him make a job change from banking to the entertainment industry.

Joanne took a temporary position as a legal secretary, which later led to an opportunity as a paralegal making $35 an hour.

Ray, a marketing executive, sent out more than 100 unsolicited resumes during a 30-day period before securing three interviews that all landed job offers.

20.7 Be good to yourself

Remind yourself of all your accomplishments—whether reworking your resume, gathering new skills, expanding your network or even landing and completing an interview. (Even if you didn't get the job, this is still an accomplishment.) Follow Susan's approach to keep your attitude positive.

Susan set up a reward system for herself. She decided to work four days a week on her job search and make Friday part of a long enjoyable weekend. On Fridays, she would either go away with friends or attend a luncheon meeting with others making a job change. At the luncheon meeting, she suggested that a prize of a free lunch be given to the person everyone agreed had had the best accomplishment that week. It became a fun activity to look forward to and motivated each person to do his or her best.

When it seems that you've done everything that you can, there is always one more thing that can be done that might make a difference. When you can't tell what it is, seek help from friends and associates, and if they have given you all the advice they can, then seek new contacts. And, in pursuing that advice, it is important to not only listen to the feedback that you receive but to be willing to make a change as a result.

Resolutions

1. Be willing to persevere—take one more step, send out one more resume, go that extra mile—because that one last step might be the one that turns the tide.

2. Make sure that your process at each important juncture of the change is the best that you can make it: You have a goal you can commit to, your resume and personal appearance are excellent, you interview well, you're trying several strategies—ads, networking, agencies, going directly to a company.

3. If you're stuck, ask for advice from friends—or consult a career counselor.

4. Learn from every situation and make the changes that feedback has shown you must be made.

5. Don't be hard on yourself. Instead, set up a reward system that reinforces the positive things you've accomplished.

6. Take time out to have fun. After all looking for a job is a job, and every job has vacation time.

Chapter 21

Where can I get more help?

21.1 Sources of employer information

As you begin your job search, you need to identify those industries as well as specific companies that would use your skills. The more information you can gather, the better. This knowledge, among other things, will help you:

- Identify specific companies you want to approach for job opportunities.

- Identify specific companies you want to approach for career information (through informational interviews).

- Learn of existing job availability within companies.

- Determine stability and growth opportunities of companies you're interested in working for.

- Tailor resumes and cover letters to their particular needs.

- Target the direct contact or most influential person in an organization.

Information on privately held companies is difficult to obtain, but publicly held companies will supply a copy of their annual report, upon request. This report usually provides an excellent overview of the company's goals and interests.

Networking (see Section 4.4) is probably one of the very best sources for obtaining information about specific companies and specific industries. The resource material listed in this section can also be very helpful and may be found in the business reference section at your public library or a college placement center. Additionally, your librarian will show you how to check for currently published information online by using one of the popular computer services.

Directories of advertisers

Standard Directory of Advertisers
National Register Pub. Co., Inc.
MacMillan Inc.
3004 Glenview Road
Wilmette, IL 60091
   Lists 24,000 companies placing national regional advertising.

Standard Directory of Advertising Agencies
National Register Pub. Co., Inc.
MacMillan Inc.
3004 Glenview Road
Wilmette, IL 60091
   Lists 4,400 U.S. and foreign agency establishments.

Directories of associations

Directory of U.S. Labor Organizations
BNA Books
Bureau of National Affairs, Inc.
1231 25th Street, NW
Washington, DC 20037
   200 national unions, professional and state employee associations engaged in labor representation.

Encyclopedia of Associations National Organizations of the U.S.
Gale Research Inc.
835 Penobscot Bldg.
Detroit, MI 48226-4094
   Lists 22,000 national non-profit organizations of all types, purposes and interest. Useful in locating placement committees, getting membership lists and learning conference dates.

National Trade and Professional Associations of the U.S.
Columbia Books, Inc.
1350 New York Ave., NW
Suite 207
Washington, DC 20005
   6,250 entries including name, year established, name of chief executive, address and phone numbers of staff members.

Directories of business organizations

Business Organizations, Agencies & Publications Directory
Gale Research Inc.
835 Penobscot Bldg.
Detroit, MI 48226-4094
   Lists business names, addresses and contact person for approximately 24,000 organizations and publications.

U.S. Industrial Directory
Cahners Publishing Company
270 Saint Paul Street
Denver, CO 80206
   50,000 company names, addresses, trade names and phone numbers of industrial entities plus local sales offices and distributors.

Directories of consultants

*Consultants and Consulting
Organizations Directory*
Gale Research Inc.
835 Penobscot Bldg.
Detroit, MI 48226-4094
　Lists more than 14,000 consulting organizations and consultants, in two volumes.

Directory of Consultants
National Association of Utility
Commissioners
Box 684
Washington, DC 20044
　Lists 190 consultants and consulting firms active in utility and transportation industries.

Corporate directories

*America's Corporate Families:
Billion Dollar Directory*
Dun & Bradstreet, Inc.
899 Eaton Avenue
Bethlehem, PA 18025-0001
　Over 8,000 major U.S. parent companies, their subsidiaries and divisions. Must have net worth of at least $500,000 to be listed.

*Best's Insurance Reports
Property and Casualty*
A.M. Best Company
Ambest Road
Oldwick, NJ 08858
　1,300 major stock and mutual property-casualty companies; 2,000 smaller casualty companies; 300 companies operating in Canada.

Directory of Corporate Affiliations
National Register Pub. Co., Inc.
MacMillan Inc.
3004 Glenview Road
Wilmette, IL 60091
　Provides detailed information on "who owns whom" as a result of mergers and acquisitions.

Directory of Executive Recruiters
Kennedy & Kennedy, Inc.
Templeton Road
Fitzwilliam, NH 03447
　Lists over 2,000 executive recruiter firms.

*Directory of Jobs and Careers
Abroad*
Vacation-Work
9 Park End Street
Oxford OS1 1HJ, England
　How to seek work abroad. Lists 500 agencies, consultants, associations, government agencies, etc. Coverage is worldwide.

*Dun & Bradstreet Million Dollar
Directory*
Dun & Bradstreet, Inc.
3 Century Drive
Parsippany, NJ 07054
　160,000 public companies in the U.S. with net worth of a half million dollars or more.

Moody's Industry Review
Moody's Investors Service, Inc.
99 Church Street
New York, NY 10007
　Ranks 4,000 leading companies in 145 industry categories according to standard financial criteria.

*Polk's Bank Directory, North
American Edition*
R. L. Polk Company
2001 Elm Hill Pike
Nashville, TN 37202
　A major detailed directory listing addresses of banks, other financial institutions and government agencies.

Pratt's Guide to Venture Capital Sources
Venture Economics, Inc.
16 Laurel Ave
Wellesley Hills, MA 02181
     More than 700 venture capital firms, corporate venture groups and small investment corporations.

Standard & Poor's Register of Corporations, Directors and Executives
25 Broadway
New York, NY 10004
     Corporate listings, directors and executives, and indexes on companies of the U.S.

Thomas Register of American Manufacturers
Thomas Publishing Co.
One Penn Plaza
New York City, NY 10019
     More than 140,000 specific product manufacturers both large and small.

Resource directories

Bureau of Labor Statistics
Inquiries & Correspondence
441 "G" Street, NW
Washington, DC 20212
     To order BLS publications.

Corporate Technology Directory
Technology Information Services, Inc.
One Market Street
Wellesley Hills, MA 02181
     25,000 corporate profiles.

Directory of American Firms Operating in Foreign Countries
World Trade Academy Press
50 E. 42nd Street
New York, NY 10017
     Lists 3,000 American corporations with factories and branch offices in 36 countries.

Directory of Industry Data Sources
Ballinger Publishing Co.
Harper & Row Publisher, Inc.
54 S. Church Street
Cambridge, MA 02138
     3,000 publishers of industry data sources.

Dun & Bradstreet Principal International Businesses
Dun & Bradstreet, Inc.
899 Eaton Avenue
Bethlehem, PA 18025-0001
     Lists nearly 50,000 prominent companies in 133 countries.

Dun & Bradstreet Reference Book of Corporate Management
Dun & Bradstreet, Inc.
899 Eaton Avenue
Bethlehem, PA 18025-0001
     Data on 200,000 presidents, officers and managers of 12,000 credit, personnel and data processing companies.

Guide to American Directories
B. Klein Publications
P.O. Box 8503
Coral Springs, FL 33065
     A listing and description of 6,000 directories with 300 major industrial, professional and mercantile classifications.

21.2 Additional help in preparing

Job hunting

101 Greatest Answers to the Toughest Interview Questions, Ron Fry, Career Press, 1994.

Adventure Careers, Alex Hiam and Susan Angle, Career Press, 1995.

Cover Letters! Cover Letters! Cover Letters!, Richard Fein, Career Press, 1994.

Finding a Job After 50, Terry and Karen Kerkstra Harty, Career Press, 1994.

From Campus to Corporation, Dr. Stephen Strasser and Dr. John Sena, Career Press, 1993.

Part-Time Careers, Joyce Hadley, Career Press, 1993.

Resumes That Knock 'em Dead, Martin John Yate, Bob Adams, Inc., 1993.

Resumes! Resumes! Resumes!, Career Press, 1995.

Successful Recareering, Joyce Schwarz, Career Press, 1993.

Take This Job and Leave It, Bill Radin, Career Press, 1993.

The Smart Woman's Guide to Interviewing and Salary Negotiation, Julie Adair King, Career Press, 1993.

The Smart Woman's Guide to Resumes and Job Hunting, Julie Adair King and Betsy Sheldon, Career Press, 1993.

What Color Is Your Parachute?, Richard Nelson Bolles, Ten Speed Press, 1995.

Where the Jobs Are, Mark Satterfield, Career Press, 1995.

Your First Interview, Ron Fry, Career Press, 1993.

Your First Job, Ron Fry, Career Press, 1993.

Your First Resume, Ron Fry, Career Press, 1992.

Consulting or business startup

101 Home Office Success Secrets, Lisa Kanarek, Career Press, 1994.

Breakaway Careers, Bill Radin, Career Press, 1994.

For Entrepreneurs Only, Wilson Harrell, Career Press, 1994.

How to Succeed as an Independent Consultant, Herman Holtz, John Wiley & Sons, Inc., 1988.

Start Up, William J. Stolze, Career Press, 1994.

The Closet Entrepreneur, Neil Balter with Carrie Shook, Career Press, 1994.

The Complete Guide to Consulting Success, Howard Shenson and Ted Nicholas, Enterprise, Dearborn, 1993.

The Home Office and Small Business Answer Book, Janet Attard, Henry Holt and Company, 1993.

The Smart Woman's Guide to Starting a Business, Vickie Montgomery, Career Press, 1994.

21.3 Business and professional organizations

Advertising and Marketing International Network
c/o Sullivan, Higdon & Sink
P.O. Box 11009
Wichita, KS 67202-0009
316-263-0124

American Accounting Association
5717 Bessie Drive
Sarasota, FL 34233-2399
813-921-7747

American Association of Engineering Societies
1111 19th St. NW, Suite 608
Washington, DC 20036-3690
202-296-2237

American Center for Design
233 E. Ontario, Suite 500
Chicago, IL 60611
312-787-2018

American Management Association
135 West 50th St.
New York, NY 10020-1201
212-586-8100

Association of Finance and Insurance Professionals
P.O. Box 212003
Bedford, TX 76095-8003
817-428-2434

Association for Systems Management
1433 W. Bagley Road
P.O. Box 38370
Cleveland, OH 44138-0370
216-243-6900

Chambers of Commerce
Local organizations are listed in business section of all telephone directories.

Institute of Real Estate Management
430 N. Michigan Ave., 7th floor
P.O. Box 109025
Chicago, IL 60610-9025
312-329-6000

National Association of Forensic Economists (NAFE)
P.O. Box 30067
Kansas City, MO 64112
816-235-1317

Women in Communications
3717 Columbia Pike, Suite 310
Arlington, VA 22204
703-920-5555

Postscript

Why does the job search process seem so long or so difficult at times? Because making a change is difficult, even when there is the reward of an attainable goal. Job change involves giving up a job you know, where you've been comfortable, and trying something different—driving a different way to work, meeting new people, being tested again, adjusting, proving yourself. But you've made successful changes before—when projects were thrust upon you, and you handled them; when responsibilities were added to your job, and you managed them; when there was a chaotic situation, and you resolved it—and you will handle the challenge of this job change just as admirably.

So look not with envy, frustration or hopelessness at another's career accomplishments, thinking, "I could never do that." But rather, be inspired. Know that as they have accomplished their goals, so will you. One of the most wonderful dynamics of this time is the river of opportunity that has been created by all the upheaval in business. There is more than enough for everyone. The river holds an opportunity that is ideal, and it is waiting for you—all you have to do is swim out after it!

A note about seminars

Over the past 10 years, thousands of individuals seeking a job and many individuals seeking to start their own businesses have benefited from my career transition seminars, entrepreneurial workshops and professional couseling.

I invite you to attend one of my seminars and accept the personal challenge of "getting the career you want with the skills you've got."

For information about public seminars for individuals or custom designed seminars for groups and corporations please write:

Ollie Stevenson
P.O. Box 16421
Beverly Hills, CA 90209-2421

Index

A

Abraham, S. Daniel, 120
Accepting offers, 186-187
Accomplishment statements,
    formulating, 22-23
Accomplishments
    activities considered as, 21-22
    analyzing, 20
    discovering your success
        pattern through, 20-24
Action verbs, 23
Activities, extracurricular, 91-93
Advice
    from contacts, 197-198
    from professionals, 198-199
Age bias, 81-100
Age Discrimination in
    Employment Act, 101
Age objections, during
    interviews, 83, 88-89
Agencies, employment, 41, 164-166
Alternatives to 9-to-5, 189-194
American Almanac of Salaries,
    42, 130, 163
Americans With Disabilities
    Act, 109ff
Angelou, Maya, 121
Appearance, 126, 128, 143
    creating a youthful, 88
    fixing, 50
    professional, 97

Aptitude, natural, 39
Attitude
    determining, 52-55
    negative, 150-151
    positive, 38-39, 48-51, 64
    team, 88

B

Barron's, 163
Bona Fide Occupational
    Qualification (BFOQ), 103
Bush, Barbara, 121
Business and professional
    organizations, 206
Business Week, 163
Buyouts and Acquisitions, 163
Buzzwords, using, 22

C

Career change, 155-160
Career goals
    alternatives, 40-42
    based on money, 39
    based on talent, 39
    based on undemonstrated
        talent, 39
    committing to, 39-50
    getting started, 37-44
    identifying, 15-36
    key steps for achieving, 38-43
    setting, 24-35

Childhood dreams, 20
Chronological resume, 81, 127, 140, 143
Cities of the United States, 163
Civil Rights Act, 101
College education, 117-124
    success without, 119-123
Competitiveness, 40
Confidence, building, 45-55, 126-127
Consulting or business startup sources, 205-206
Consulting, 189, 193
Contacts, 60-67
    letters, 63-67
Contract positions, 52, 54
Corporate directories, 203
Cover letter, 143
Craig, Jenny, 120
Criminal record, handling, 149-150

D

Day-care services, 74
Degree, success without, 119-123
Directories
    corporate, 203
    of advertisers, 202
    of associations, 202
    of business organizations, 202
    of consultants, 203
    resource, 204
Disabled employees, 109-115
Discrimination, of minorities, 104-107
Divorce, returning to work after, 71, 125
Downsizing, 57-64
Dreams, childhood, 20

E

Education
    acquiring additional, 196
    college, 117-124
    for career changes, 155-156
Elder care for parents, 74
Employee fee-paid agencies, 166
Employer fee-paid agencies, 166
Employer information, sources, 201-204
Encyclopedia of Associations, 42, 92, 99, 163
Equal Employment Opportunity Act, 101
Equal Employment Opportunity Commission (EEOC), 101, 106, 114
Equal Pay Act, 101
Ethnicity, problems with, 101-107
Experience, lack of paid, 125, 196
Expert advice, seeking, 198-199

F

Failures, handling, 147-154
Family, unsupportive, 48-49
Fear, 45-55
Feedback from others, 20
50 Fabulous Places to Raise Your Family, 163
Filling a need, 113-134
Finding the right job fit, 18-19
Fitting in, 93
Five-second interviews, 42
Flexibility in the workplace, 74
Flexible plan for growth, 43-44
Flextime, 74
Forbes, 163
Fortune, 163
Freelancing, 189, 191-192
Friends, making, 50
Functional resume, 60, 70-71, 82, 123, 128, 140, 158

G

Gates, Bill, 119

Gender, problems with, 69-79
Geographic economic
    indicators, 163
Getting started, 37-44

H

Hispanic Alliance, 107
Home-based business, 189-190

I

Illnesses, 110
Image
    creating a youthful, 83, 87-89
    professional, 97
Income information, 42
Independent contracting, 189,
    192-193
Industry buzzwords, using, 22
Information interviews, 41,
    62-64
Insecurity, 45-55
International Toastmaster's,
    91-92
Interpersonal skills, 28
Interviewing, 47, 52, 54
    with more than one company,
        184-185
Interviews
    age objections during, 83,
        88-89
    five-second, 42
    handling questions about
        age, 88-89, 97-99
    handling questions about
        disabilities, 112-114
    handling questions about
        ethnicity, 102-104
    information, 41, 62-64
    long-distance, 167
    networking, 62-64, 67
    preparing for, 96-97

revealing salary
    information, 176-177
role-playing, 70
tips for returning to the work
    force, 126-130
tips for technical
    employees, 143-144
tips for women, 70-71, 75-76

J

Jennings, Peter, 121
Jewish Defense League, 107
Job Accommodation Network, 114
Job goals, broadening, 134-135
Job guides, 163
Job hopping, 71
Job hunting sources, 205
Job Offers, 183-187
Job Seeker's Guide, the, 163
Job sharing, 74
Job transfers, 48, 52, 54

K

Karan, Donna, 120
King, Larry, 121

L

Layoffs, 57-64
    counseling for, 58
    dealing with on your
        resume, 59-60
    networking after, 60-67
    reacting to, 58
    stigma of, 57-58
    telling creditors about, 59
    telling family about, 58
    telling friends and associates
        about, 59
    telling prospective employers
        about, 59
Leadership skills, 28
Letters, networking, 63-67

Limiting yourself, 17-18
Long-distance interviewing, 167

M

Making changes, 196
Managerial/administrative
    skills, 28
Marketable skills, identifying,
    125-126
Marshall, Penny, 121
Mental body, fixing, 50
Mentors, 47, 60
Minority discrimination, 104-107
Minority employees, 101-107
Mistakes, handling
    past, 147-154
Money, 163
Moore, Michael, 121

N

NAACP, 107
Nation's Business, 163
*National Business Employment
    Weekly,* 163-164
National Information Center for
    Independent Living, 114
National Institute of Disability
    and Rehabilitation Research,
    114
Negative reputation, 150-151
Negotiation, salary, 74, 177-180
Networking, 40-42, 47, 60-67,
    92-93, 127, 134, 156, 158,
    164, 180, 197
    interviews, 62-64, 67
    letters, 63-67
Newspaper ads, responding
    to, 41

O

*Occupational Compensation
    Survey,* 130, 163

Offers
    accepting, 186-187
    getting in writing, 184
    negotiating, 184
Older employees, 81-90
100 Black Men, 102
Opportunities, 47-48, 93,
    136-137
Organizations, business and
    professional, 206
Outplacement services, 58

P

Part-time jobs, 189ff
Perdue, Frank, 120
Personal traits, 28
Personal values, 33
Physical body, fixing, 50
Planning to succeed, 37-38
Positions, contract, 52, 54
Positive attitude, 38-39
Problems, resolving, 152-153
Promotion, 53, 55

Q

Questions
    about age, 88-89, 97-99
    about disabilities, 112-113
    about ethnicity, 102-104
    asked of women, 72-73

R

Rejection, 195-196, 199
Relocating, 52, 54, 71, 161-170
Reputation, negative, 150-151
Researching companies, 88,
    95-96, 129
Resolving problems, 152-153
Resource directories, 204
Responsibility, receiving
    more, 55

Resumes
addressing layoffs on, 59-60
age mentioned on, 81
chronological format, 81,
127, 140, 143
critiques on, 62
education mentioned
on, 82-83
for inexperienced
employees, 92-94
for minorities, 101-102
for returning to the work
force, 78-79
for technical employees,
139-143
functional format, 60, 70-71,
82, 123, 128, 140, 158
job-hopper's, 77
lack of paid experience on,
127-128
making youthful, 83-87
personal details on, 70
preparing, 41
writing for relocation,
166-167
Returning to work after an
absence, 71-72, 125-131
Rights
of minorities, 101ff
of the disabled, 109-114
Role-playing interviews, 70

S

Salaries, 42, 53, 55, 95, 130,
171-181
compensation packages, 178
negotiating, 74, 177-180
women's, 73-74
Salary cuts, 173-174
Salary guides, 163
Salary information,
revealing, 174-177
Selling yourself short, 17-18

Skills
determining worth of, 42
interpersonal, 28
leadership, 28
managerial/administrative,
28
market value of, 73-74, 95,
171-181
natural, 39
recognizing value of, 45-46
updating, 196
Small Business
Administration, 194
Solomon, Russell, 120
Sources
consulting or business
startup, 205-206
job hunting, 205
Special Needs Information
Referral Center, 114
Spiritual body, fixing, 49-50
Spouses, 71
Success pattern, discovering,
20-24
Success, fear of, 48-49

T

Talent
choosing a goal based on, 39
discovering, 20
following, 15-17
Technical employees, 139-146
Telecommuting, 74, 189-191
Temping, 189, 192
Temporary agencies, 156, 166
Tompkins, Susie, 120
Traits, personal, 28
Transfers, job, 48, 52, 54
Tuition reimbursement,
company programs, 118-119
Turner, Ted, 120

U

Unsoeld, Jolene, 121

V

Values, personal, 33
Verbs, action, 23
Vernon, Lillian, 120
Volunteering, 39, 41, 91-92,
    125-126, 157-158

W

Wall Street Journal, the, 41,
    136, 163-164

Women
    dealing with spouse's
        relocations, 71
    employment of, 69-79
    handling difficult interview
        questions, 72-73
    interview tips for, 70-71, 75-76
    quoting salaries, 73-74
    returning to work after an
        absence, 71-72, 125-131

Y

Younger employees, 91-100